BUSINESS
GREATEST HITS

Also by Kevin Duncan

Marketing Greatest Hits
Run Your Own Business
Small Business Survival
So What?
Start
Tick Achieve

BUSINESS GREATEST HITS

A MASTERCLASS IN MODERN BUSINESS IDEAS

KEVIN DUNCAN

A & C Black • London

First published in Great Britain 2010 & reprinted 2011

A & C Black Publishers Ltd
36 Soho Square, London W1D 3QY
www.acblack.com

A CIP record for this book is available from the British Library.

ISBN: 978-1-4081-2643-1

This book is produced using paper that is made from wood grown in
managed, sustainable forests. It is natural, renewable and recyclable.
The logging and manufacturing processes conform to the
environmental regulations of the country of origin.

Design by Fiona Pike, Pike Design, Winchester
Cartoons by Gray Jolliffe
Typeset by Saxon Graphics Ltd, Derby
Printed in Croatia by Zrinski

As always, my writing is dedicated to my girls:
Sarah, Rosanna and Shaunagh

Acknowledgements

My heartfelt thanks to Gordon Wise for the introduction, and to Lisa Carden for helping it all along.

Cartoons by Gray Jolliffe.

For regular free updates and new material visit kevinduncan.typepad.com/greatest_hits or contact the author at:

kevinduncan@expertadvice.co.uk
expertadviceonline.com

To purchase the Apps of this book, or its sister title *Marketing Greatest Hits*, visit:

www.businessgreatesthits.com
www.marketinggreatesthits.com

CONTENTS

OVERVIEW

What's the book all about?

This book attempts to summarise the top 40 best pieces of business thinking in recent times to give you a breadth of knowledge at your fingertips. It is designed to be the definitive compendium of everything you need to know from the best minds in modern business – abridged, condensed, and ready for immediate action.

Modern business is a blur of jargon with thousands of books all purporting to hold the key to relentless success. The working reality is often very different. I have distilled all the books into one-minute summaries and interlinked them with six short, explanatory chapters so that you can become an authority and decide for yourself.

As well as saving hundreds of hours of reading time, the reader should be able to grasp ideas with pithy accuracy, explain them authoritatively to colleagues and, crucially, avoid being hoodwinked by those who claim to understand a concept when in fact they have got the wrong end of the stick.

You need no longer be afraid to get to the point quickly. You can draw together the most important ideas using some basic unifying principles such as:

- **Big theories are not necessarily complicated – this book makes sense of them for you.**

- **Simple ideas always work – you can apply them immediately to your business.**

- **Broad and often misused concepts can be clarified and demystified.**

- **What is business strategy? There is no mystery and plain language reveals all.**

- **Treat case histories with extreme caution. If they were that easy, everyone would be doing it.**

- **Make sense of all the jargon and buzzwords.**

How is it organised?

I have corralled 40 of the most interesting books into six sections covering the big themes, business strategy, leadership, business classics, creativity, and organisation. If you want to get to grips with one of these areas in particular, then head straight to that section. If you prefer a more sequential approach, then work your way through from the beginning. Although business is never chronological, you will at least be able to absorb the most popular current concepts, take a view on the issues, examine the vexed area of creativity, and then decide how to get sufficiently organised to enact some of it.

The six sections

There's no such thing as right and wrong in business. It's all a matter of opinion. As a result, there are potentially only two ways to determine what the 'right' business strategy is:

- **the most senior person in the room says so;**

- **the person writing the case history retrospectively decrees that it was, when in fact it was probably luck.**

In the spirit of the second point, I have used a healthy dose of my own opinion to decide which books make the cut to appear within these pages. I have chosen them either because they are widely acknowledged to be seminal works, or because they represent a particular stance or counterpoint to the prevailing view. As such, they may not all be the *most* famous, but they will offer contrasting views so that you can be aware of all the angles in a particular debate. I will be delighted if you disagree with my selections because this will mean that you are already reading widely and forming your own opinions.

Black swans and flat worlds: the big themes

In Chapter 1 we grapple with some of the big themes in modern business, and arguably there is no bigger question in business, or indeed life, than: is there a pattern or is everything random? We examine *Fooled by Randomness* by Nassim Nicholas Taleb, and use another of his books, *The Black Swan,* to show how relying on what you think you know could well be a dangerous game.

A huge proportion of business success or failure is determined by the power of context, so we use *Outliers* by

Malcolm Gladwell, and *Freakonomics* by Levitt & Dubner to investigate this tricky area, often with surprising results.

How much of a push do people need in order for them to realise their business ambitions? Thaler & Sunstein think they need a *Nudge*, and Brafman & Brafman think you can *Sway* them. We will take some potentially tricky economic theory and put it through the blender so we can all understand it.

Has the Internet changed everything? Some say no – it's just another medium or route to market and should be viewed in context alongside all the others. Others regard it as totally world-changing, particularly Tapscott & Williams, the authors of *Wikinomics.*

We finish up the first chapter with a robust analysis of *The World is Flat* by Thomas L. Friedman, who believes that the fall of communism and the rise of the Internet have removed pretty much every previous political and geographical barrier to doing business. Global influences on local business, and vice versa, are a hot topic.

Questions, lies and the tiger that isn't: business strategy unravelled

Chapter 2 gets its hands dirty with business strategy and data. The macho old school approach with its underlying theme of world domination receives a thorough going over when we look at *Sun Tzu: The Art of War for Executives* by Donald Krause. We debate whether business approaches really do need to be that aggressive.

Can you condense business strategy down to just one question? Fred Reichheld says you can in his book *The Ultimate Question*, so we examine his proposed method and you can draw your own conclusion. What happens when businesses give away their products for free? It changes pretty much every business model you thought might be relevant, according to Chris Anderson in *Free*, his follow-up to *The Long Tail* (reviewed in the companion to this book, *Marketing Greatest Hits*, A & C Black, 2010).

Most businesses these days have collected so much data that they don't know what to do with it. Part of the knack is knowing how to organise it, so we draw advice from two Edward de Bono books, *Six Thinking Hats* and *Six Frames*.

Seeing a pattern of stripes in the leaves, we would run from what looks like a tiger. There are illusions in numbers too, often just as intimidating, according to Blastland & Dilnot. They explain the important art of how not to be fooled by data and jargon in *The Tiger That Isn't*, whilst *Liar's Paradise* by Graham Edmonds exposes some of the worst excesses of modern businesses and equips us with the power to spot poor corporate behaviour.

We round off the chapter with a broad contextual view on *The Logic of Life* with Tim Harford, the self-styled undercover economist, in a wide-ranging attempt to understand why people make the decisions they do.

Screw it, let's do it: the elusive art of leadership

Chapter 3 looks at leadership. Fewer subjects have vexed businesspeople more. How do you do it? How do you define and measure it? Can you follow any guidelines? It's like grasping at fog or nailing jelly to the wall. So we start with a very fair question: *Why Should Anyone Be Led By You?* It's the title of a book by Goffee & Jones, and a very good place to start examining this very tricky area.

Drawing the received wisdom together is a difficult task, but one that I have relished. There are many possible sources, so I have cast the net wide to encompass as many opinions as possible: *How to Lead,* by Jo Owen, *Smart Leadership,* by Yudelowitz, Koch & Field, and *Leadership for Dummies,* by Loeb & Kindel.

Of course, there is considerable disagreement on what makes a great leader, and some reject the bulk of conventional thinking, so we investigate how to be a maverick leader with Ricardo Semler, a self-styled anti-establishment businessman from Brazil, and author of *The Seven-Day Weekend.*

It's good to know what all the available wisdom suggests, but there's nothing like applying your own style and just getting on with it, according to Richard Branson in *Screw it, Let's Do it.*

The classics: old hat or still relevant?

Chapter 4 looks at the oldest chestnut in business: is the thinking espoused by the grand masters still spot on, or is it old hat that has been superseded by digital media and a plethora of modern thinkers? We start by examining the lessons from the best-run companies in the world, courtesy of *In Search of Excellence,* by Peters & Waterman. It was published in 1982 and is still revered in many a boardroom, along with *Built to Last* (Collins & Porras), and *Good to Great* (Jim Collins). Between 1994 and 2001, Jim Collins became famous for shattering myths and ensuring the long-term success of companies, but he still couldn't work out which book should have come first, as we shall see.

A contrary view is provided in *The Halo Effect,* by Phil Rosenzweig, who claims that all this supposed fact is no more reliable than storytelling. If it were that easy to simply copy what successful companies are up to, then everyone would be doing it.

John Harvey-Jones became famous for using his intuition and *Making it Happen,* so we run the rule over his work philosophy before delving into some alternative views and the prospect of a twisted future (in which we have since arrived), with Charles Handy in *The Age of Unreason.*

Creativity: can you learn it?

One of the most discussed areas of business in recent times has been that of creativity. So in Chapter 5 we ask some critical questions. Can you define it? How do you keep having good ideas that will make your business a success? If you or your company is not that creative, can you make them more so? How different minds work may hold some clues, so we start by investigating *A Whole New Mind* by Daniel H. Pink.

Suggested methods for encouraging creativity are forthcoming in *See Feel Think Do* by Milligan & Smith, so we'll look at whether some element of technique can unlock the creative door. Randomness is good too, according to Seth Godin in *Purple Cow,* and the late Paul Arden in *Whatever You Think, Think the Opposite.*

Embracing new ideas is the key to it, according to Clay Shirky, author of *Here Comes Everybody,* a comprehensive rundown on how the Internet has revolutionised the marketplace for ideas, and peoples' ability to publish them without fear of failure.

Organisation: how to get on with it

In Chapter 6 we sweep all this together: big themes, strategy, leadership approaches and creativity. None of it matters unless you or your company can get on and enact it. That requires good organisation, and as the old joke goes, most organisations are not that well organised. We start with the rather alarming question: why bother? *Hello Laziness* by Corinne Maier, explains how you should do as little as possible, whilst Tom Hodgkinson tells us *How to be Idle.*

Working on the assumption that being indolent isn't necessarily the way forward, we examine how large companies should do it in *Execution* by Bossidy & Charan. There are salutary lessons to be learned here. How small companies do it, or should do it, is completely different, as explained by Simon Tupman in *Why Entrepreneurs Should Eat Bananas.*

Then we get up close and personal by looking at how you can do it yourself, with *Getting Things Done* by David Allen, and *How to Get More Done* by Fergus O'Connell. As a final flourish, we look at getting your attitude right with Paul McGee, whose acronym *S.U.M.O.* stands for *Shut Up, Move On.*

And finally...

Although the points in the books are often contradictory, we draw all the one-sentence summaries together to form an intriguing business manifesto to inspire your approach.

"All those in favour of getting a Tarot reader in, say 'Aye'."

CHAPTER 1.
BLACK SWANS AND FLAT WORLDS: THE BIG THEMES

Is there a pattern or is everything random?

Fooled By Randomness Nassim Nicholas Taleb

"Supposing a tree fell down, Pooh, when we were underneath it?"

"Supposing it didn't," said Pooh after careful thought,"

Winnie the Pooh

Let's dive straight in and grapple with the big one: do things happen for a reason or are they intrinsically random? Nassim Nicholas Taleb caused a sensation in 2004 when he published *Fooled by Randomness.* The book is all about how we perceive 'luck' in our personal and professional lives. We often hear that an entrepreneur has 'vision' or that a trader is 'talented' but all too often their performance is down to chance, not skill. Perhaps not surprisingly, there are many in the business world who simply don't want to admit such a possibility. Surely all the successes in life are down to the skill and professionalism of the enactor?

Of course everyone wants to succeed, but what causes some people to be more successful than others? Is it really down to skill and strategy, or something altogether more unpredictable? It's the latter, according to Taleb, but unfortunately most of us fail to understand probability and so continue to believe that events are non-random, finding reasons where none exist. As such, he believes that many rich people are just lucky idiots, so there is no point in looking for inspiration in their stories because there is no cause and effect.

He introduces the idea of Black Swans, which are unexpected random events. These are based on the philosopher John Stuart Mill's assertion that no amount of observation of white swans can prove that all swans are white – the sighting of a single black swan can disprove it. For example, seeing George Bush alive many times does not prove that he is immortal. This simple point has crucial implications for the manner in which we look at business events and data.

This is not a textbook, but there are many thought-provoking messages in it:

1. **Journalists are bred to not understand randomness**
   They feel they must have a reason for everything, but often there isn't one.

2. **The noise in markets usually disguises the signal**
   Aberrations draw attention but distract from the true underlying information.

3. **Because a rich person can lose it all, they cannot be said to be truly happy until their life is finished**
   This observation was made by the Greek legislator Solon when he claimed to be unimpressed by Croesus, supposedly the richest person ever.

4. **The Monte Carlo Simulator simulates random occurrences**
   This is a computer programme that runs rather like extended Russian roulette. Examining its behaviour makes nonsense of most so-called patterns in market analysis.

5. **Those predicting events usually don't know what they are talking about**
   They don't know what can sensibly be deduced from the data they have, and so make incorrect claims and assumptions.

6. **There is usually no link between the most recent event and the one about to happen**
   This is crucial when analysing trends.

This is heavy-duty stuff. No one wants to admit that things might happen regardless of their efforts, so the assertions made here amount to tough medicine for many – in particular control freaks, egotists and those prone to machismo.

The one-sentence summary

Don't fool yourself: much business performance is down to chance, not skill.

The book is quite long and highly technical, so it is not for the faint-hearted, despite having sold huge numbers and being translated into 18 languages. Although the author quite enjoys being a bit obscure, he does use clear examples, and the fact that the reader needs to work a bit to get into the subject matter probably reflects the fact that he is so much more intelligent than the rest of us. The central message, however, is fundamental to businesses, many of which probably believe that they have more bearing on their markets than they really do. Let's push this idea a bit further.

Relying on what you think you know: a dangerous game?

The Black Swan NASSIM NICHOLAS TALEB

Three years later (2007) Taleb was developing his ideas even further in *The Black Swan*. Everything is essentially random, he says. Black Swans (unpredictable events) disprove everything we think we know from time to time and that's a fact of life. Thousands of instances of one thing do not disprove the possibility of another, so we should stop seeing patterns where there might not be any. In this respect, relying on what we think we know could well be a dangerous game because we might be fundamentally wrong whilst firmly believing that we are right. This combination of conviction and fallacy could be very nasty in any context, and could certainly have serious implications for action taken in the business world.

As well as repeating the story that everyone assumed all swans were white until overseas travel revealed black ones, he introduces other analogies. A turkey is fed for 1,000 days before Christmas – then it is killed. Once again, all previous experience would suggest one thing but actually this has no bearing on the next event. It is easier to predict how an ice cube would melt into a puddle than guess the shape of an ice cube by looking at a puddle. Too many people, and businesses, confuse cause and effect.

The impact of Black Swans is huge, they are near impossible to predict, and yet afterwards we always try to rationalise them – an essentially pointless exercise. Many businesses embark on intensive witch-hunts when something goes wrong when they might be better off admitting it was a random event and getting on with the next thing.

The highly expected *not happening* is also a Black Swan. How often does a business predict something that never actually happens? The answer is: all the time. One only has to look at the annual forecast to see that.

The one-sentence summary
Ignore the experts, stop trying to predict everything, and embrace uncertainty.

We can learn from some important lessons in the book:

1. **We focus on small parts of what we know and use them to project what we don't (often incorrectly)**
   This is both misleading and unhelpful.

2. **We use narrative fallacy (stories) to fool ourselves with reasons that aren't there**
   This is similar to the point made in *The Halo Effect* by Phil Rosenzweig in Chapter 4.

3. **We behave as if Black Swans don't exist – they clearly do**
   Admitting to the presence and possibility of randomness would help take the pressure off many a business.

4. **What we see is not necessarily all there is**
   Consider what you don't know.

5. **Variability matters**
   'Don't cross a river if it is four feet deep on average.'

You cannot approach this book like a dip-in textbook, but sticking with the narrative can be highly rewarding because it is rich in anecdote and analogy. These include Umberto Eco's *anti-library*. He has 30,000 books in his personal collection – a huge number – but they are far less useful than the books he does not have. It's what you haven't read, and what you do not know, that makes the difference. This may well contain a salutary lesson for businesses. What problems could be better handled if companies asked themselves what they do *not* know?

Mediocristan is a land where everything is averaged and so unhelpful to the point of meaninglessness. He urges all concerned to avoid this unhelpful mythical place. *Extremistan* is where all the learning is. This is where one single observation can disproportionately affect the aggregate or the total. So it may be time to re-evaluate what you think you know. Do you really know it to be true? Have you simply been rearranging your prejudices and fooling yourself that you have been thinking carefully? Many businesses would appear to do this frequently, often unintentionally. Sometimes, it all depends on the context in which the problem is being analysed.

The power of context: how strong is it?

Outliers MALCOLM GLADWELL
Freakonomics LEVITT & DUBNER

Malcolm Gladwell has become one of the most famous authors on social commentary. In 2008 he published his third book *Outliers*. (If you want to look at what he said in the others, do look at the sister book to this one, *Marketing Greatest Hits*, A & C Black, 2010). His view is that when we try to understand success, we normally start with the wrong question. We ask *What is the person like?* when we should really ask *Where are they from?* He says that the real secret of success turns out to be surprisingly simple, and it hinges on a few crucial twists in people's life stories – on the culture they grow up in and the way they spend their time.

An outlier is a statistical observation that is markedly different in value from the others in the sample – tiny influences have made certain people 'special'.

Opportunity is the first crucial element of being successful at anything. *Legacy* is the second – behaviour handed down over many generations that dictates the way that people react to circumstances. He cites many examples to demonstrate the point. They include:

1. **Countries with subservient cultures have pilots involved in more plane crashes**
   This is because the co-pilots do not impose on their superiors – sometimes not even making emergencies evident to air traffic control.

2. **Easterners have a stronger work ethic**
   As such, they are better at maths because they are used to taking a lot of time to solve problems.

3. **Top sportsmen are born at the beginning of the year**
   As youngsters they start a little bigger, and are then given the best training and the most practice.

4. **The best in any field have exceeded 10,000 hours of practice**
   This means that those who start late at something do not usually achieve the very best.

5. **Social class has nothing to do with intelligence**
   That is, until the ability to study, revise, or practice starts to disadvantage those less privileged.

Fans of determinism will approve of this book, since it verifies that your success is determined by where you come from and what happens on the way. It is not strictly an academic book. It is more a series of interesting anecdotes that make a general point. Although it challenges you to make the most of your own potential, in practice the reader cannot change their circumstances, time of birth, where they come from, or any other major factors other than pure hard work. The first half of the book *(Opportunity)* explains the origin of outliers. The second half *(Legacy)* is only tenuously related to it – it is more an explanation of cultural differences.

The one-sentence summary
Context is absolutely crucial: what appears to be a reason for something rarely is.

Hold that thought whilst we look at the contents of *Freakonomics* by Levitt & Dubner, first published in 2005, and still topical five years later. This is a case of an economist and an inquisitive journalist exploring the hidden side of everything. They find links and patterns in all sorts of strange areas by asking unconventional questions such as:

- **What do estate agents and the Ku Klux Klan have in common?**

- **Why do drug dealers live with their mothers?**

- **How can your name affect how well you do in life?**

Their view is that by using information about the world around us we can get to the heart of what is really going on. We need to be much more inquisitive and not accept received wisdom because there is usually much more to it. Indeed, if you follow the thinking behind the whole book, you will probably never take anything for granted again. What appears to be a reason for something rarely is – instead it is often a twisted piece of received wisdom that everyone blindly accepts.

Let's take an example. Parents prevent their child from going to play in a house where a gun is kept, but allow them to visit another friend who has a swimming pool. In fact the odds are 1:11,000 of drowning and 1:1 million of gun death. In other words, we are all terrible risk assessors, and as a result, we often make very dim decisions that fly in the face of the facts. Put another way, there is a massive difference between correlation (two things appear to be linked) and causality (one actually causes the other). We need to distinguish between the two to make sensible decisions.

In the broadest sense, the book has nothing to do with business. However, the enlightened mind can take the principles and apply them to the discernment of truly relevant data, and the kind of inquisitiveness that is essential for any successful strategy. Many business decisions are based on strategic howlers and inaccurate thinking – and human behaviour is one of the most fraught areas, because people do some very strange things. Businesses are constantly struggling to understand their motivations, and what messages and methods are going to influence their actions.

How much of a push do people need?

Nudge THALER & SUNSTEIN
Sway BRAFMAN & BRAFMAN
In 2008, two books emerged which grappled with rationality and decision making. Thaler & Sunstein suggested that governments could improve people's decisions about health,

wealth and happiness by giving them a *Nudge*, while the Brafmans explained how the irresistible pull of irrational behaviour causes people to *Sway*. Both theories have significant implications for businesses.

Nudge is a discussion of how we can apply the new science of choice architecture (the discipline of designing and arranging systems and services that require choices by customers) to nudge people towards decisions that will improve their lives by making them healthier, wealthier, and freer. The book is much loved by politicians because it adds modernity and legitimacy to what could otherwise be criticised as blanket social engineering. The book, however, is keen to emphasise that it is, politically, neither left nor right.

The fact is that every day we make decisions on a huge range of topics such as personal investments, schooling and what our children eat. Unfortunately, we often choose poorly. If we take our 'humanness' as a given, we can understand how people think and design choice environments that make it easier for people to decide what is best for them – a nudge in the right direction without restricting freedom of choice.

There are scores of examples from everyday life that make the point. A director of food services in schools can increase or decrease the consumption of various (potentially more healthy) foods by as much as 25 per cent simply by rearranging their position in the cafeteria. Behavioural economists borrow from psychology in recognising that the mind can fool itself. In a visual context, we are quite capable of looking at an image of two identically sized tables and being convinced that one is bigger than the other.

The ability to be so 'smart and dumb' at the same time can be attributed to our *Automatic System* (instinct rather than actively thinking) versus our *Reflective System* (more deliberate and self-conscious). There is a rather contrived acronym to remember the main themes:

i*N*centives: people have to feel they are getting something for their choice

***U*nderstand mappings: you have to understand how people see things**

***D*efaults: make sure the 'do nothing' route is one of the best**

***G*ive feedback: investigate the rejected options and experiment with them**

***E*xpect error: humans make mistakes, so well-designed systems allow for this**

***S*tructure complex choices: if it's difficult, break it down into easier chunks**

This book is what might be called a 'medium' read. Some would call it heavy economic theory, while others consider it a welcome relief from much denser academic material. Either way, it provides stimulating angles for those in business confronted by important choice architecture issues.

The one-sentence summary
People will make irrational decisions if left to their own devices.

Meanwhile, Brafman & Brafman were pointing out that we usually think we are rational beings but the science of decision-making would suggest otherwise. Logical thought can be subverted or 'swayed' in many ways. Irrational behaviour can be perpetrated by the most experienced and well-trained people, including pilots and doctors. Common reasons are:

- **Overreacting to a potential loss**

- **Taking dangerous risks when a lot is at stake**

- **Refusing to withdraw even with a small loss**

- **Misjudging something because it is in the wrong context**

- **Being prejudiced by prior information**

Our brains have two different parts that are constantly struggling with each other: the 'pleasure centre' wild side that gets a kick out of taking risks, shopping, winning money and so on, and the 'altruism centre' that wants to do the best for others and always seeks reasonable compromise. Sometimes it just doesn't seem worth the bother to dissent from the prevailing view, so many people stay quiet when the majority has got it wrong – particularly for an easier time at work.

There are scores of examples from anthropology, aviation, sports and politics to illustrate the points they make, and the narrative rolls along nicely, more in the style of a story than a textbook.

The thesis is a useful complement to, and development of, many other social theory books of recent times: *Freakonomics, Nudge, Herd,* and *The Tipping Point.* (Summaries of the last two can be found in the sister book to this one, *Marketing Greatest Hits*, A & C Black, 2010). It is this very similarity of material that makes it potentially confusing for anyone who reads several of them. A shorthand for separating the thinking in each book is:

Freakonomics
Patterns of social behaviour can be rooted in linked causes.

Herd
Huge numbers of people simply copy each other because they are social.

The Tipping Point
Little things can make a big difference.

Nudge
Providing different options or small incentives can change mass behaviour.

Sway
Irrational behaviour can affect even the best trained and the most experienced people.

One thing unifies them all, and that is that people are without doubt strange beasts who do odd things. But they also do some wonderful things, and are capable of extraordinary mass effort, especially when given the means with which to do so. Arguably no greater opportunity has arisen for mass collaboration than that of the invention of the Internet.

Global influences on local business

The World is Flat THOMAS L. FRIEDMAN

In 2005 Thomas L. Friedman produced his masterpiece *The World is Flat*. Knowledge and resources are connecting all over the world, effectively flattening it, he claimed. These forces, which include blogging, online encyclopedias and podcasting can be a force for good – for business, the environment and people everywhere. He reckoned there are ten forces that flattened the world:

1. **11th September 1989**
   The day the Berlin Wall came down an extra three billion consumers entered the world, effectively doubling the size of the world from a business perspective.

2. **8th September 1995**
   The launch of the World Wide Web.

3. **Workflow Software**
   Making stuff happen much more seamlessly.

4. **Uploading**
   Everybody can now contribute to online communities.

5. **Outsourcing**
   Your company may not need to do much of what it sells to customers.

6. **Offshoring**
   For example, many US services are provided in India.

7. **Supply-chaining**
   Making sure everything arrives in the right place, fast.

8. **Insourcing**
   For example, UPS repair all of Toshiba's laptops.

9. **In-forming**
   Google, Yahoo! and MSN searches inform people at the touch of a button.

10. The steroids

Digital, mobile, personal, and virtual devices all fuel the machine.

He also outlines The Triple Convergence. This is where new players, a new playing field, and new processes all come together in 'horizontal collaboration'. This is a superb synthesis of all the developments you can think of in modern communications, and it walked away with the *Financial Times &* Goldman Sachs Business Book of the Year award.

Many of the elements of globalisation are recorded in a fragmented way, so it is difficult for businesses to keep tabs on them all. Here they are all drawn together in one place. It is very thought-provoking because it highlights how recent so many of the developments we now take for granted are. Things are changing fast, so what you thought you knew last week may not be true or relevant today. There are lots of anecdotes and examples to bring the drier technological points to life, and it would take a bold person to attempt to draw together all the thinking in one sentence. That is, however, the purpose of this book, so I will humbly have a go.

The one-sentence summary

The Internet has effectively flattened the world to the point where businesses can view the entire thing as both a potential resource and a market.

There we are, I did it. Six hundred pages of beautifully researched narrative condensed into twenty-five words. This book is very long, so you need a bit of stamina to get through it, but it's worth it because the implications are enormous. Old-fashioned 'local' boundaries have effectively gone out of the window, giving way to a huge world market with near-endless possibilities. Businesses can capitalise on this phenomenon or fall prey to it depending on their approach, their speed of response, and their attitude to new technology.

Has the Internet changed everything?

Wikinomics TAPSCOTT & WILLIAMS

It certainly has, argued Tapscott & Williams a year later in *Wikinomics* (2006). Mass collaboration changes everything, and this is because the knowledge, resources and computing power of billions of people are self-organising into a massive, new collective force. Interconnected and orchestrated via blogs, wikis, chat rooms, peer-to-peer networks and personal broadcasting, the Web is being reinvented to provide the world's first global platform for collaboration.

Peer production is what happens when masses of people and firms collaborate openly to drive innovation. There are many weapons of mass collaboration – free telephony, open source software, global outsourcing platforms, and so on. For example, Procter & Gamble now has 90,000 registered scientists who give them ideas but are not on the payroll, courtesy of their InnoCentive marketplace. Traditional companies used to be highly secretive (the 'locked filing cabinet' syndrome) and P&G were notorious for this for years. Now they can benefit from the four principles of Wikinomics, which are:

1. Being open

Operate with candour, transparency and access.

2. Peering
The opposite of command and control: egalitarianism is the watchword.

3. Sharing
Smart companies treat intellectual property like a mutual fund.

4. Acting globally
The business world is now effectively borderless, so you need to act as well as think globally.

Wikinomics is defined as a perfect storm in which technology, demographics and global economics create an unrelenting force for innovation and change. The Net generation does not passively receive messages – it wants to search, scrutinise, authenticate, collaborate and organise everything. 'N Gen' norms are speed, freedom, openness, innovation, mobility and playfulness.

The ideas keep coming. Coase's Law from 1937 (a firm will expand until transaction costs reach those of the open market) now needs to be viewed backwards (firms should shrink until transaction costs no longer exceed the cost of doing it externally). An Ideagora is a marketplace for ideas, based on the agoras that were the centre of politics and commerce in ancient Athens. The benefits of peer production are harnessing external talent, keeping up with users, boosting demand for complementary offerings, reducing costs, shifting the locus of competition, taking the friction out of collaboration, and developing social capital.

As a result of all this coordinated effort, the stock of human knowledge now doubles every five years. Virtually all of Google's new product ideas come from the 20 per cent of time staff are required to take off for 'goofing around', but Tarzan economics means that many businesses cling on to the vine of the old before they embrace the new.

The one-sentence summary
The Internet has changed everything, so you need to open up your business to your customers.

This is quite a lot to take in, and the book is fairly long and detailed so you have to dig hard for the nuggets. So what should we make of it all? First of all, businesses must accept that the world has changed, so labouring on with the old methods won't work. Secondly, there is a need to embrace change, but it needs to be the right change. Simply bolting on 'a bit of that online stuff' will not do. If necessary, whole elements of the business may need to be re-engineered to achieve a decent result. Thirdly, the good news is that the effort of customers can be harnessed to produce spectacular results. This is not cynical exploitation. Consumers have more power and expression than ever, and are eminently capable of making their views and actions known without any help from companies. They are intrinsically interested in joining in, and will 'reward' those businesses that open up and deal with them in an open and honest way.

CHAPTER 1 WISDOM

- Don't fool yourself: much business performance is down to chance, not skill.

- Ignore the experts, stop trying to protect everything, and embrace uncertainty.

- Context is absolutely crucial: what appears to be a reason for something rarely is.

- People will make irrational decisions if left to their own devices.

- The Internet has effectively flattened the world to the point where businesses can view the entire thing as both a potential resource and a market.

- The Internet has changed everything, so you need to open up your business to your customers.

"How's your thinking hat doing? Mine hasn't come up with anything."

CHAPTER 2. QUESTIONS, LIES AND THE TIGER THAT ISN'T: BUSINESS STRATEGY UNRAVELLED

The macho old school approach and world domination

Sun Tzu: The Art of War for Executives DONALD KRAUSE

The language of business has borrowed wantonly from the world of the military. Businesses launch campaigns, fight battles, deploy tactics, send the troops in, provide air cover, attack on several fronts, storm the barricades and frequently claim that it's a jungle out there. Where did all this belligerence come from? Well, one culprit is undoubtedly the military strategist Sun Tzu, or at least his disciples. He lived in north east of China 2,500 years ago, around the same time as Confucius. In truth though, we shouldn't be too harsh on him, because there is no direct evidence that he ever wrote down any of his thoughts. It was in fact probably done about 100 years later when another warlord called Cao Cao carefully annotated a text based on his teachings.

Anyway, it wasn't until 1996 that Donald Krause morphed it into *The Art of War for Executives,* suggesting that the wisdom of this ancient text is invaluable commentary on such topics as leadership, strategy, organisation, competition and co-operation. It may well be but, as with all information, it has to be in the hands of the right students. Assuming you are not about to invade a country yourself, consider his 10 principles for competitive success:

1. **Learn to fight**
   A nice passive start. He regards competition as inevitable but warns against seeking it for its own sake.

2. **Show the way**
   Leadership determines success, and is achieved

through self-discipline, purpose, accomplishment, responsibility, knowledge and example.

3. **Do it right**
   All competitive advantage is based on effective execution.

4. **Know the facts**
   To achieve success, you must manage information well.

5. **Expect the worst**
   Do not assume the competition will not attack – instead, rely on adequate preparation to defeat the opposition.

6. **Seize the day**
   The most important success factor is speed, and quick victory is the aim of competitive action.

7. **Burn the bridges**
   Position yourself where there is a danger of failing. When people are unified in their purpose, no obstacle can stand in their way.

8. **Do it better**
   Combine expected and unexpected tactics – the latter are more powerful when applied judiciously.

9. **Pull together**
   Organisation, training and communication are the foundations of success.

10. **Keep them guessing**
    The best competitive strategies have no form – they are so subtle that no one can discern them.

If taken the wrong way, the whole idea of comparing war with business could lead to overly macho approaches, and arguably this has already happened the world over. If you dig deep, this is not really what the book is all about, but you can see how certain elements have been extracted and willfully made to appear pugnacious. Have a look at the list of principles. Whilst regarding competition as inevitable, Krause warns against seeking it for its own sake. Many modern businesses would benefit from not antagonising their competitors. The burning bridges concept has been much abused too. 'Failure isn't an option' has become a rallying call in macho companies, but it is clearly nonsense because so many businesses do fail. So all this has to be treated with a pinch of salt.

In truth, the overall message in the book is: 'Do not engage the enemy unless it is absolutely necessary.' In other words, this is as much a book about the *avoidance* of war as the *enactment* of it. As such, I have plumped for this non-aggressive interpretation of the advice in it.

The one-sentence summary
Concentrate on what you are going to do and don't become obsessed with the competition.

It is certainly interesting to apply the teachings of an ancient war expert to business and view the advice in a modern context, as long as the transference of knowledge across the ages is done with a light touch. The interpretations are clear enough to be easily transferable to business matters, and there are clear sections on planning, competitive strategy, conflict, control, positioning, flexibility and reputation. There is also a lot on using spies for information, which is clearly illegal and so cannot be endorsed in the modern world. Perhaps not surprisingly given its origin, the competition is generally referred to as 'the enemy', which is pushing the language too far in a business context. Most level-headed businesspeople would argue that it is more profitable to concentrate on what *you* are going to do, rather than become obsessed with the opposition.

Can you condense business strategy down to just one question?

The Ultimate Question FRED REICHHELD

Once you have investigated the world domination option, why not try to discover the meaning of life (and business?), or at the very least distil it down to one sentence? *The Ultimate Question* by Fred Reichheld (2006) claimed to do just that. One of the biggest problems for businesses today is the presence of too much data. It sounds strange, but in the rush to find out as much as possible about markets and customers, most companies end up with too much information. As a result, they become blinded and often don't know which measures are the ones that really matter.

The author (who works at Bain & Co., the management consultants) believes it is possible to turn customers into promoters by asking and tracking one simple question: *Would you recommend us to a friend?* From this, a Net Promoter Score (NPS) can be calculated. Increasing this by 12 points versus a competitor can double a company's growth rate. The equation is simple: P - D = NPS, where P are promoters and D are detractors. In other words, you want to have more fans than grumblers.

The question is certainly simple and based on extensive research, and there is compelling evidence here that loyalty is the key to profitable growth. On a 10 point scale from extremely likely to not at all likely (to recommend), promoters must score nine or 10, passives seven to eight, and detractors six or below. Promoters are beneficial to businesses because:

1. **They have a higher retention rate**
   Detractors defect at higher rates.

2. **Margins**
   Promoters are less price-sensitive.

3. **Annual spend**
   Promoters increase their purchases more rapidly.

4. **Cost efficiencies**
   Detractors complain more frequently.

5. **Word of mouth**
   Positive referrals come from promoters, while detractors are responsible for 90 per cent of negative comments.

All of this sounds like so much common sense, but perhaps the crucial point is that the book offers a quantitative system for measuring these notoriously difficult areas. However, this type of measurement cannot just be superimposed at short notice – a company would have to embrace the methodology over a decent period of time and keep a close eye on the scores. That would require money and patience. For those with the resources and time, according to the author, this system works better than standard satisfaction surveys, which fail because:

1. **Too many surveys, too many questions**
   Many people suffer from survey fatigue, and most are too long.

2. **The wrong customers respond**
   Do you want a genuinely random sample, or the opinions of your most profitable customers?

3. **Employees don't know how to take corrective action**
   They know what's wrong, but they don't know what to do about it.

4. **Too many are marketing campaigns in disguise**
   Loaded questions and surveys that are precursors to a sales call distort the value of research.

5. **The scores don't link to economics**
   The link between satisfaction scores and customer behaviour that drives profitability is tenuous at best.

6. **Plain vanilla solutions can't meet companies' unique needs**
   Too many questionnaires are off the peg and don't suit the job.

7. **There are no generally accepted standards**
   There are dozens of different satisfaction metrics so they are almost impossible to compare.

8. **Surveys confuse transactions with relationships**
   Are you measuring one interaction or the whole relationship?

9. **Satisfaction surveys dissatisfy customers**
   Business executives don't like to be disturbed, but they are happy to disturb their own customers.

10. Gaming and manipulation wrecks their credibility
   If staff are rewarded because of high customer satisfaction scores, then the scores become an end in their own right – a case of hit the target but miss the point.

The one-sentence summary
Customers who are prepared to recommend your product or service are the ultimate barometer of success.

Too many companies are addicted to bad profits. These are corporate steroids that boost short-term earnings but which burn out employees and alienate customers. They undermine growth by creating legions of detractors – customers who sully the firm's reputation and switch to competitors at the earliest opportunity. Instead, you are better off ensuring that you monitor carefully whether your customers are prepared to recommend you or not, and take the necessary action to make sure that they are as happy as possible.

What happens when businesses give away their products for free?

Free CHRIS ANDERSON
Here's a weird area: giving your products away for free. It's not as odd or suicidal as you might think, and lots of companies do it, according to Chris Anderson in the book of the same name (2009). His contention is that old economic certainties are being undermined by a growing flood of free goods – the germ of an idea he began in his previous book

The Long Tail. This has become possible because production and distribution costs in many sectors have plummeted to unthinkable levels.

The flexibility of the online world allows producers to trade ever more creatively, offering items for free to make real or perceived gains elsewhere. As an increasing number of things become freely available, our decisions to make use of them are determined by the popular reputation of what's on offer and the time we have available for it. This is quite different from old-fashioned price-based supply and demand models.

So in the future when we talk of the money economy, we will really be talking about the reputation and time economy. The original loss leader concept is giving away one thing to get another: the Internet has taken this to a new level. There are now essentially three prices: something, nothing (free) and less than nothing – this is negative price, where you get paid to use a product. For example, there is a gym in Denmark where you pay nothing as long as you go at least once a week.

He describes the economics of atoms, which is based on tangible items. The economics of bits is based on storage space and is intangible, leading to 'freeconomics' (a semantic nod to the book we looked at in the previous chapter). By way of illustration, he refers to Seth Godin's *Unleashing the Ideavirus,* which reveals that 20 years ago all of the top 100 companies in the Fortune 500 either dug something out of the ground or turned a natural resource into something you could hold. There are now only 32 – the others sell ideas.

The one-sentence summary
The Internet has turned traditional economics upside down by making many things free, so look carefully at your reputation and the time you demand from your customers.

Information wants to be free, as stated in the 'hacker ethic' defined by Stephen Levy in 1984:

- **Access to computers should be unlimited and total**
- **Always yield to the Hands-on Imperative**
- **All information should be free**
- **Mistrust authority – promote decentralisation**
- **Hackers should be judged by their hacking**
- **You can create art and beauty on a computer**
- **Computers can change your life for the better**

There's more: the demand you get at a price of zero is many times higher than at a very low price – the 'penny gap' identified by Josh Kopelman. In other words, there are only two markets: free, and everything else. This means that the demand curve isn't curved, and your traditional pricing strategy may well be wrong. Modern business models should therefore build a community around free information, use it to design something that people want, let those with more money buy more polished versions of the product, and keep repeating the process. He also introduces 10 principles of Abundance Thinking:

1. **If it's digital, sooner or later it's going to be Free.**

2. **Atoms would like to be Free too.**

3. **You can't stop Free.**

4. **You can make money from Free.**

5. **Redefine your market.**

6. **Round down.**

7. **Sooner or later you will compete with Free.**

8. **Embrace waste.**

9. **Free makes other things more valuable.**

10. **Manage for abundance, not scarcity.**

There is much to ponder here about modern markets. Understandably, the book takes a fairly extreme position on the subject, stretching a point to make it. Taking all this at face value could frighten the living daylights out of more traditional marketers, so a more balanced view may be needed. Start by understanding the points about free markets, and consider how elements of this ultra-modern approach could affect, or be harnessed by, your business.

How to organise your information

Six Thinking Hats EDWARD DE BONO
Six Frames EDWARD DE BONO
Edward de Bono is one of the undisputed heroes of thinking techniques, so now we look at two of his books: the classic *Six Thinking Hats*, first published in 1985, and the much more recent *Six Frames* (2008). Both are important with regard to how to generate constructive thought, and how to

organise information. De Bono's six thinking hats technique has become one of the most successful approaches to business thinking ever. The six hat types are:

1. **White hat**

   Facts, figures, information.

2. **Red hat**

   Emotions, feelings, intuition, hunches.

3. **Black hat**

   Cautious and careful (beware overuse).

4. **Yellow hat**

   Speculative positive, benefit-led, constructive.

5. **Green hat**

   Creative, lateral, provocative.

6. **Blue hat**

   Control, structuring, organisation.

The technique forces people to adopt different attitudes and approaches to thinking, which is intended to remove them from bias and politics. If followed correctly, the six hats provide an element of process to what can otherwise be a random brainstorm or ideas session. In subsequent versions of the book, de Bono noted with some dismay that the method was often used incorrectly, in that one individual often wore the same hat for the whole meeting. In fact, everyone should wear each hat simultaneously to make best use of everyone's intelligence and experience. As some of the novelty of using the process has worn off, and business techniques have developed, the system has attracted some criticism. '*It is not a complete solution*,' claim Yudelowitz, Koch & Field (see next chapter).

There may be two reasons for this:

1. **Six frames of thinking are probably too many for most people to remember accurately**
   The vast majority of business people are unable to name all six colours of hat, let alone their designation and function.

2. **It is hard for people to adopt another mode of thinking, let alone six**
   Some people are so set in their ways that they are unable to fully enact a different character type, even for a short period.

The one-sentence summary
Discipline your business thinking, and the way in which you organise information.

Six Frames (for thinking about information) came out in 2008. In a world saturated with facts and figures as never before, how do we focus our attention to make the most of information at our fingertips? The book suggests a 'six frames' technique to help direct our attention in a conscious manner, rather than always letting it get pulled to the unusual and irrelevant. Just as we can decide to look north, west or even south-east, so we can set up a framework for directing our attention and interpreting information. The six frames are:

1. **Purpose: the triangle frame**
   To emphasise the huge importance of being clear and laying out the exact basis of your need for information.

2. **Accuracy: the circle frame**
   To direct your attention specifically to the accuracy of the information at which you are looking.

3. **Point of view: the square frame**
   To assess the information for neutrality and look at it in different ways.

4. **Interest: the heart frame**
   To direct attention to matters of interest rather than the pure need for information.

5. **Value: the diamond frame**
   A summary or overview that determines the value of the information.

6. **Outcome: the slab frame**
   The outcome and conclusion. This is particularly crucial because not everyone faced with the same information comes to the same conclusion.

We cannot live without information and we are surrounded by it. But it can often become overwhelming to the point where it loses its usefulness. Companies and individuals who are in this position would do well to clarify and simplify it long these lines. The big enemy of good thinking is confusion, which becomes more likely the more active the mind. Clarity is good, but not at the expense of comprehensiveness. The main cause of confusion is trying to do everything at once. The system makes this an orderly process. The book is short and simple, but it should not be applied simplistically, so care and attention is needed, especially when dealing with complex issues or large amounts of potentially daunting data.

Lies, damned lies and statistics: how not to be fooled by data and jargon

Liar's Paradise GRAHAM EDMONDS
The Tiger That Isn't BLASTLAND & DILNOT

We'll start with the stark view and then try to make some sense of it. Graham Edmonds launched *Liar's Paradise* on the world in 2006, and hit businesses with some fairly chunky accusations. He claimed that 80 per cent of companies think that they are fraud free, but that a recent survey (conducted by PriceWaterhouseCoopers) actually revealed fraud in 45 per cent of them. He suggested that there are seven degrees of deceit:

1. **White lie**
   Told to make someone feel better or to avoid embarrassment.

2. **Fib**
   Relatively insignificant, such as excuses and exaggerations.

3. **Blatant**
   Whoppers used when covering up mistakes or apportioning blame.

4. **Bullshit**
   A mixture of those above combined with spin and bluff to give the best impression.

5. **Political**

    Similar to bullshit but with much bigger scale and profile.

6. **Criminal**

    Illegal acts from fraud to murder, and their subsequent denial.

7. **Ultimate**

    So large that it must be true. As Joseph Goebbels said: *'If you tell a lie big enough and keep repeating it, people will eventually come to believe it.'*

In a way this view confirms what all cynics suspect – that the workplace constantly bombards us with lies, fakery and spin. Case histories of Enron, Boo.com, the European Union and others provide the proof on a grand scale, and deconstructions of other levels of lying help the reader to navigate their way through the day-to-day types. You can then decide how to react. It has tips on how to suck up to the boss, pass the buck and endure meetings, and every businessperson should read the chapter on Lies and Leadership. Interesting quotations include:

'The truth is more important than the facts.' FRANK LLOYD WRIGHT

'Those that think it is permissible to tell white lies soon grow colour-blind.' AUSTIN O'MALLEY

'Honesty may be the best policy, but it's important to remember that apparently, by elimination, dishonesty is the second-best policy.' GEORGE CARLIN

The book essentially condemns most corporate cultures and so needs to be viewed lightly by those who have to work in them. You can't run around with a jaundiced view all day and expect to be fulfilled and effective. Indeed, there is a moral dilemma lurking within: do you tell the truth and get trodden on, or join the liars?

The one-sentence summary
Treat information with great suspicion until you know the real story.

A different take on how to see through a world of data, in this case mainly numbers, was provided by Blastland & Dilnot in *The Tiger That Isn't,* first published in 2007. Seeing a pattern of stripes in the leaves, we would run from what looks like a tiger. There are illusions in numbers too, often just as intimidating. The book reveals what the numbers really show, and exposes the tiger that isn't. Life comes in numbers: public spending, health risks, who is rich and poor, the best and worst schools and of course, business information. The trick to seeing through them is to apply the lessons of your own experience, and investigate them more thoroughly.

The book works through most of the ways in which numbers can be presented, and shows how to make sense of them, using lots of examples from everyday news stories. Specifically relevant to business are:

1. **Counting**
   Counting things is very difficult, and the results are often wrong.

2. **Chance**

   Frequently things are truly random, but we still look for patterns (remember the Black Swans in the previous chapter?).

3. **Up and down**

   Numbers go one way or the other, regardless of what you do.

4. **Averages**

   Disguise huge variation and squeeze everything into a mass.

5. **Targets**

   What they do not measure is as important as what they do.

6. **Risk**

   All that matters is what it means to you.

7. **Sampling**

   If the sample is flawed, then so is the conclusion.

8. **Data**

   They are often plain wrong, so be careful when drawing conclusions.

9. **Shock figures**

   These are more likely to be wrong or misinterpreted than shocking.

10. **Comparison**

    Mind the gap – they might not be comparable.

11. **Correlation**

    This is not the same as causation – there may be no link between the two numbers.

In truth, everyone should read this book as a sanity check on the numbers we have thrown at us or bandy around ourselves – particularly politicians and journalists. We are all guilty in one way or another, but businesses must be very careful if they start to believe information that is in fact wrong, because this could lead to a nasty chain of decisions, all of them flawed. We all have to deal with numbers, but if you don't understand them then at the very least make sure that you do not misrepresent them.

Why people make the decisions they do

The Logic of Life TIM HARFORD

We round off this chapter with a look at *The Logic of Life* by Tim Harford (2008). If humans are so clever, why do we smoke and gamble, or take drugs and fall in love? Is this really rational behaviour? And how come your idiot boss is so overpaid? In fact, Harford believes, the behaviour of even the unlikeliest of individuals complies with economic logic, taking into account future costs and benefits, even though we don't quite realise it.

Rational choice theory affects most things, and can sit happily even with the most passionate emotions. Most things can be explained: overpaid (apparently useless) bosses, proximity to neighbours, racism, and divorce decisions, among others. Rational people respond to incentives: when it becomes more costly to do something, they will tend to do less. In weighing up their choices, they will bear in mind the constraints on them, and their total budget. And they will consider the future consequences of present choices. This applies just as much to prostitutes and criminals as it does to anyone else.

The idea that everybody responds to incentives and consequences may have wider application than we think. Game theory (originally posited by Von Neumann) uses rational decision making to analyse every decision in a way that should lead to calmer, more beneficial decisions, but it is hard for the layperson to implement. Most of us just follow the 'wisdom of crowds' principle, but don't adjust our guesses. In truth, human interactions are so shot through with ambiguity that they are better viewed as focal points (according to Schelling). For example, when confronted with the issue of where and when would two people who can't talk meet each other in New York tomorrow? Everyone agrees it should be under the clock at Grand Central Terminal at noon.

The logic of life is often not logical. Tournament theory means that workers sabotage one another to win the top job: the bigger the boss's pay, and the less they have to do to earn it, the bigger the motivation for everyone else to aim for it. On a personal level 'egonomics' is mental civil war: should I smoke or not? All humans wrestle with such conflict. And the 'death of distance' doesn't make the world flatter, it makes it spikier, with evermore activity taking place in cities – centres of innovation and idea exchange. The more people cluster together like this the faster the rate of technological progress – currently we should have a world-beating idea every two months (one per billion people per year).

The one-sentence summary
Every human being, no matter how diverse, complies with economic logic.

It's a messy old world, but you can make some sense of it. Good information, calm reflection and an inquisitive approach all help. Not everything is what it seems at first and so careful exploration may well be required. Then, once you have decided what to do, you need to think about how to persuade everyone else to do what you want. That's what we'll look at next.

CHAPTER 2 WISDOM

- **Concentrate on what you are going to do and don't become obsessed with the competition.**

- **Customers who are prepared to recommend your product or service are the ultimate barometer of success.**

- **The Internet has turned traditional economics upside down by making many things free, so look carefully at your reputation and the time you demand from your customers.**

- **Discipline your business thinking and the way in which you organise information.**

- **Treat information with great suspicion until you know the real story.**

- **Every human being, no matter how diverse, complies with economic logic.**

"I'm starting to lose confidence in our leadership."

CHAPTER 3.
SCREW IT, LET'S DO IT: THE ELUSIVE ART OF LEADERSHIP

Let's start with a fair question

Why Should Anyone Be Led By You? GOFFEE & JONES

Tap the word 'leadership' into a popular search engine and you will be confronted by 122 million possible answers. No wonder people find the whole area confusing. This is another Holy Grail of the business world, and arguably one that has been analysed to death. This will not, however, prevent us from dedicating a whole chapter to it. Let's start with what appears to be a very fair question for anyone aspiring to lead the troops: Why should anyone be led by you? Goffee & Jones first posed the question in 2006.

Their assertion was that simply copying how other leaders behave will not necessarily make you a good leader – very much the major criticism of business books that suggest that, if you follow what the successful companies have done, then yours will be successful too. Life's not like that and if it really were that simple then everyone would follow the golden rules and we would all be a roaring success.

Instead, they suggested that great leaders essentially act as 'authentic chameleons', consistently displaying their true selves through different contexts that require them to play a variety of roles. Leadership is situational, non-hierarchical and relational, and it can come from within an organisation just as easily as from the very top. There are various things you can do to help increase the chances of being a decent leader. These include identifying personal attributes that will have meaning for followers, exposing strengths and weaknesses effectively, improving their ability to read and shape context, recognising when and where to make compromises, identifying communication channels that work, and understanding and delivering on what followers need.

If this list doesn't sound that startling, then maybe the whole business of leadership has been shrouded in too much mystique. A recurring theme of the writing in this area is that simple home truths serve the top leaders better than anything more complicated. The book is well written and based on 25 years of research, so the advice comes from a broad base. Its overall orientation adds a dose of humility to the often rather macho area of leadership, and, on the face of it, it should be reasonably easy enough to follow the steps that they recommend (assuming you have the desire):

1. **Be yourself – more – with skill**
   Leadership needs to be situational, non-hierarchical and relational.

2. **Know and show yourself – enough**
   You need a clear sense of who you are, and the confidence to bare all.

3. **Take personal risks**
   You can't expect everyone else to go out on a limb if you won't.

4. **Read – and rewrite – the context**
   Leadership is contextual, so you need to study and adjust the context in which you operate.

5. **Remain authentic – but conform enough**
   Stay true to your character, identify enough with the old ways, but remain sufficiently distinctive to engineer change where it is needed.

6. **Manage social distance**

   You need to evoke high levels of loyalty and affection, but this should be laced with tough love. You can get close to the troops, but not too close.

7. **Communicate – with care**

   Skilful leaders use the right mode of communication, not just the right message.

The one-sentence summary

To be a good leader you have to earn respect.

Although this summary may at first appear overly simplistic, there is a universal truth to it. Dictatorial leaders are not generally effective, and these days the views of everyone need careful consideration. Followers are also discussed in the book (you can't have leaders without them). Followers want authenticity, to feel significant, a sense of excitement and to be part of a community. And in these days of open communication, you can be sure that they will let you know fast and furiously if they are not happy with your style.

Of course, leadership has a price as well as a prize – there are no easy answers, you can be easily undone and when things go wrong it's your fault, so aspirant leaders should be careful about pursuing status for the sake of it. Overall, the question in the title is the strongest point, albeit somewhat rhetorical and circular. Anyone who desires to be a leader should certainly ask it of themselves, and see what they come up with. If they are found wanting, then the principles and experience here should help, but don't fall into the trap of assuming you can be a great leader when you might not necessarily have those types of qualities.

Are some leaders smarter than others?

Smart Leadership YUDELOWITZ, KOCH & FIELD
Well we have to ask the question don't we? Given the huge number of companies that go completely off the rails, it stands to reason that many leaders aren't actually that good, and are probably not that clever. Without going into huge detail about how on earth incompetent people rise to the top, we can at least look at the qualities of intelligence that should be appropriate for the people in charge. Yudelowitz, Koch & Field looked at this in *Smart Leadership,* first published in 2002.

The authors have three main influences; psychologists and other leadership writers, writers with unusual insights and philosophers who have pondered the human condition. That's not a bad breadth of opinion with which to create a melting pot of helpful knowledge on the subject. They describe the point of leadership as being 'to initiate change and make it feel like progress.' Change would appear to be a perpetual theme of leadership and coping with it seems equally as important as dictating and directing it. Whilst this book is a synthesis rather than a clearly delineated point of view, six main themes do emerge:

1. **Leaders need to adopt a cause but should not plan the future**

   Set a direction, but don't assume that it will remain the case.

2. **Leadership is not always necessary**

   The need for it varies over time – sometimes things just work well anyway.

3. **Leadership is a culture, not a person**
   You can't have one leader and thousands of followers
   – many have to get involved.

4. **Managers achieve objectives. Leaders work to a purpose**
   They are not the same thing.

5. **Managers defer decisions. Leaders take them**
   Being decisive is better than inactivity.

6. **Don't be too consensual about consensus**
   Listen to the facts. Hear their opinions. Then decide.

The one-sentence summary
Smart leaders set a course, assume it will change, and try to get lots of people to show leadership qualities.

The book is full of good advice and inspiring quotes such as:

'Leadership is a potent combination of strategy and character. But if you must be without one, be without the strategy.'

'Now that I am CEO, what am I supposed to do?'

'The only real training for leadership is leadership.'

'Leadership has a harder job to do than just choose sides. It must bring sides together.'

The Triangle of Tensions is a smart concept that summarises the struggle of leaders well. Its three components are:

1. **The Individual Identity**
   Who the leader really is: their past and their emotional compass.

2. **The Canned Role**
   The formal expectations as defined by future expectations and rational elements.

3. **The Emergent Process**
   This is the messy reality of the present, and all the associated politics.

Who'd want to be a leader pulled in these three quite different directions every working day? These tensions represent a constant struggle for any leader, and personal mastery of this is only achieved via Learner Leadership, a never-ending circle of self-awareness, learning, judging, acting and mobilising, according to the authors. So your true self will be constantly wrestling with what is expected of you and the messy truth of how the company is doing. This phenomenon never goes away, and needs to be embraced fully in order for a leader to be genuinely effective. Indeed, leadership is full of paradoxes, which include:

- **Leadership requires intelligence and self-awareness, but the two are rarely combined, and the latter is often elusive;**

- **A strong ego is necessary for confidence, but also prevents you from appreciating what's really going on;**

- **Leaders should be both guileless and artful;**

- **Leaders need to confront anxieties that others would rather sweep under the carpet, yet this is the last thing people want from their leaders.**

So there you have it: an enigma wrapped in a riddle. To aspire to a leadership role is to seek uncertainty and a box of bombs in your in-tray every morning. It certainly isn't for the faint-hearted. And to cap it all, the authors claim that it is impossible to have too much leadership in an organisation, which begs the question: if everyone were a leader, then who would be following?

Drawing the received wisdom together

How to Lead Jo OWEN
Leadership for Dummies LOEB & KINDEL

Digging deeper into the leadership problem, it becomes more and more apparent that there is no single source of wisdom. Rather like the principle of this volume, it might be better to draw widely from many sources so that you can synthesise your own version of how it might work for you. Two other books do just that: *How to Lead* by Jo Owen (2005) and *Leadership for Dummies* by Loeb & Kindel (1999). As we are beginning to see, good wisdom in this area is probably timeless.

The first book contains all the important stuff you need to know about leading well: motivating people, building networks, selling ideas, influencing people, giving feedback, evaluating people, and learning to be lucky, if that's possible. Apparently, luck is normally down to practice, persistence and perspective, although many might not agree. It takes you through the foundations, practice and mastering of leadership, and makes the point that leaders aren't necessarily at the top of organisations, which rings a loud bell from other sources in this chapter.

The main leadership qualities fall into focusing on people, being positive and being professional (that means having loyalty, honesty, reliability, solutions and energy). Leading from the middle involves finding your way through the matrix, which is the nasty 'adminisphere' in the middle of all companies that have grown beyond a certain size. Those who tend to fall by the way are: the expert (technically competent, but that's all); cave dweller (territorial); politician (political); boy scout (naive) and autocrat (acts as though they already are a leader). None of these types generally make it to the top, so it might be worth asking yourself whether you fall into any of these categories.

A survey of 700 leaders reveals the qualities that they look for in emerging leaders: adaptability, self-confidence, proactivity, reliability and ambition. These are presumably easier to claim than to enact, otherwise we'd all be at the top. There is also an interesting checklist of what people want from a good boss:

- **they show an interest in my career;**

- **I trust them – they are honest with me;**

- **I know where we are going and how to get there;**

- **I am doing a worthwhile job;**

- **I am recognised for my contribution.**

There are good quotes to be had here:

'Many sins are forgivable, but disloyalty is not one of them.'

'An organisation full of Ghengis Khan wannabes is unlikely to be a happy place.'

'It is possible to learn leadership. If you know how to, you are well on the way to success.'

The one-sentence summary
Successful leaders will take on risk, change and ambiguity.

In the second book, Loeb & Kindel don't adopt any particular philosophical stance – they simply attempt to guide us through all the important aspects of leadership, such as what it takes to be one and how to enact it. According to them, you become a leader by acting like a leader. There are a number of desirable traits in potential leaders, which include:

- 'Stick-to-itiveness' – patience, repetition and learning. 'Err and err and err again, but less and less and less'. – Piet Hein, Danish poet and mathematician

- Imagination can help turn randomness into a vision, and all leaders need it

- Leadership is stewardship, which means you are assuming a set of responsibilities, not getting your title carved in stone

- The final test of a leader is that they leave behind in other people the will and conviction to carry on

The book includes an interesting debate around the axioms of leadership. The German word for management is *Führungskunst,* which means 'the art of leadership'. In most countries management and leadership are viewed as being different things. *'Each one teach one'* refers to the ability to spread leadership qualities around teams, although no book has ever completely resolved the issue of whether absolutely anyone can show leadership qualities or not.

It outlines 10 qualities of a true leader: eagerness, cheerfulness, honesty, resourcefulness, persuasiveness, co-operation, altruism, courage, supportiveness and assertiveness. You have to wonder whether such a superhuman exists anywhere. This is rapidly followed by 10 ways to master leadership skills: preparing, volunteering, keeping an open mind, giving speeches, developing discipline, meeting deadlines, staying in touch, listening, co-operating and doing things for others. Again, anyone feeling perfect today? So if you don't happen to have those 20 characteristics at your disposal this week, you might want to give that bid for promotion a miss.

How to be a maverick leader

The Seven-Day Weekend RICARDO SEMLER
Right. That's quite enough of all the earnest stuff about how to be a brilliant leader. There is always another way for those of us who can't match up to perfection every moment of the working day. You've guessed it: act like a maverick and do what you want. That's the message in *The Seven-Day Weekend* by Ricardo Semler, first published in 2003. Indeed, his previous book was called *Maverick!* and sold 1.1 million copies. The author runs a huge number of companies in Brazil, and insists on working in an unconventional way. He likes to question everything:

- **Why are we able to answer emails on Sundays, but unable to go to the movies on Monday afternoons?**

- **Why do we think the opposite of work is leisure, when in fact it is idleness?**

- **Why doesn't money buy success if almost everyone measures their success in cash?**

- **Why does our customised and carefully crafted credo look like everyone else's?**

- **Why do we think intuition is so valuable and unique – and find no place for it as an official business instrument?**

And so on. Subtitled *The Wisdom Revolution: Finding the Work/Life Balance,* the book rails against the 21st-century phenomenon of 'work anywhere', and suggests that it's just not necessary. The author's company Semco sustained a 40-fold increase in size using a host of peculiar working practices that would have many a conventional company running for the hills. The book contains lots of ideas for maintaining staff loyalty and interest such as:

1. **Retire a little**
   Take Friday afternoons off and offset it against retirement age.

2. **Up 'n Down Pay**
   Vary hours and pay to suit your circumstances.

3. **Work 'n Stop**
   Take long periods off but declare your intention to return.

4. **Unconventional board meetings**
   Always have two vacancies for any members of staff that want to attend.

The one-sentence summary
If in doubt, trust everyone and do nothing.

Many companies rather suspiciously view democracy and freedom as alternative methods of running a business, but at Semco they form the heart of how business is done. One piece of reverse psychology suggests that when anything untoward happens you should do nothing on the assumption that good sense will eventually sort it out, assuming you have employed sensible grown-ups. All this from a company where workers choose their bosses, financial information is shared with everyone and a high percentage of the employees determine their own salaries. The net effect is that, in the main, self-managed teams replace hierarchy and procedure.

The book gives you an authoritative source on which to base radical ideas so that you can challenge staid working practices or conservative thinking. It contains lots of novel ideas and some catchy phrases such as 'corporate yo-yo dieting' – the boom and bust cycles that companies always get themselves into, but which can generally be avoided if the management pays proper attention. There are also some neat little tricks that you can implement straight away, such as always asking why three times in a row.

So there's an alternative view that leaves us with something of a dilemma: do we draw all the conventional wisdom together and apply it to the letter, or do we celebrate individualism and let everything take its course? Admittedly, the author has only ever run his own company so he can only speak from that experience. He is probably quite unconventional to work with, so not all of his ideas could necessarily be implemented without causing havoc in most conventional companies. Not that that would necessarily be a bad thing. Many old-style organisations are trying hard to introduce greater elements of personal freedom, and reward individual initiative. Semler was probably ahead of his time in 2003, and arguably remains so.

Applying your own style

Screw it, Let's Do it RICHARD BRANSON

Of course, justifying flying by the seat of your pants and letting your style do the talking is far easier if you are a roaring success, which is where we come to the iconic Mr Branson. Many a maverick has crashed and burned, and taken the subsequent flak from critics accusing them of being far too flamboyant and cavalier. But when they get it right, their personal and company style is often described as being mercurial, inspirational, visionary, and even possessing genius. Winners are always blessed with brilliance, according to business folklore.

Well maybe, maybe not. In truth, this is, like so many case histories, often fanciful storytelling long after the harsh reality. As Richard Branson is the first to point out, the road to success is littered with calamity, and it is only the tenacity to keep trying that eventually gets a result. His book *Screw it, Let's Do it,* published in 2006, admirably gets to grips with the rather more prosaic truth.

According to Branson's philosophy, simple truths in life and the right attitude can inspire and enable you to do practically anything. People will always try to talk you out of ideas and say, 'It can't be done', but if you have faith in yourself, it almost always can. The author has certainly made plenty of mistakes and taken a lot of risks, so this is not just a 'plain sailing' manual by someone who has led a charmed life.

The main principles of just do it – have fun, be bold, challenge yourself and live the moment – are all solid, inspirational stuff. There are also much softer principles such as value family and friends, have respect for people and do some good for others. You can dip in pretty much anywhere and grab a motivational thought in ten seconds. Choose from:

- **Believe it can be done**

- **Never give up**

- **Have faith in yourself**

- **When it's not fun, move on**

- **Have no regrets**

- **Keep your word**

- **Aim high**

- **Try new things**

- **Love life and live it to the full**

- **Chase your dreams but live in the real world**

- **Face problems head on**

- **Money is for making the right things happen**

- **Make a difference and help others**

Possibly the most striking feature of such a list is its humility. Some business leaders have caught the bravado bug, and tend to embark on relentless soapboxing about how their gung ho approach beat the company into shape. There is no sign of that here, which makes the ideas all the more applicable to a wider range of circumstances, including small businesses and personal life.

The one-sentence summary

People will always tell you it can't be done, but if you have faith in yourself, it almost always can.

This is a short, inspiring book, and you can read it in a couple of hours. The author struggled with mild dyslexia at school, so it is more a stream of consciousness, or a selection of sound bites, than finely honed prose. No matter. The message comes across loud and clear. As ever, the only small health warning is that it always seems easier for someone who has 'done it' to reflect back on the hard times – but it is doubtless harder to apply that philosophy when you are actually struggling right now.

So that's leadership for you. Another case of grasping at fog to see if you can emulate the great success stories? Yes and no. There seems little doubt that the keen student could read widely in this area and learn much. Those of us who aren't naturals could probably improve to one degree or another. But the debate will always remain that you've either 'got it' or you haven't, and no amount of reading can give you that.

CHAPTER 3 WISDOM

- To be a good leader you have to earn respect.

- Smart leaders set a course, assume it will change, and try to get lots of people to show leadership qualities.

- Successful leaders will take on risk, change and ambiguity.

- If in doubt, trust everyone and do nothing.

- People will always tell you it can't be done, but if you have faith in yourself, it almost always can.

"You're going to just love these new stats — we made them up last night."

CHAPTER 4.
THE CLASSICS:
OLD HAT OR STILL
RELEVANT?

Lessons from the best-run companies

In Search of Excellence PETERS & WATERMAN

Now we come to the mighty titans of the business writing world. These are the kinds of names and book titles that you'll hear bandied around in hushed tones in boardrooms the world over. Names like Peters, Collins and Handy, those who command messianic respect on the speaker's podium at deadly-serious business conferences from Miami to Mumbai. With sales well into the millions, the common or garden businessperson like you or me might be forgiven for wondering what all the fuss is about. Can it really be true that these people, above all others, have a grip on wisdom in business that the rest of us can only marvel at? Now's the time to have a detailed look.

We'll start with the classic *In Search of Excellence* by Peters & Waterman, first published in 1982. Tom Peters has been described by *The Economist* as the 'über-guru of business', and by the *Los Angeles Times* as 'the father of the post-modern corporation.' You can't get higher praise than that. So what is he saying about businesses? Well, he and his co-author outline eight basic principles of how to run a successful business and stay ahead of the competition. These are:

1. **A bias for action**

   Get out there and try something. Even if the action you take is ultimately unsuccessful, it's better than doing nothing.

2. **Stay close to the customer**

   Don't be distracted by the internal stuff. In far too many companies the customer has become a nuisance whose unpredictable behaviour damages carefully laid strategic plans.

3. **Autonomy and entrepreneurship**
   Even if you're big, act small. The most discouraging fact of big corporate life is the lack of what made them big in the first place: innovation.

4. **Productivity through people**
   That's all companies are made of, so trust the people you work with.

5. **Hands-on, value-driven**
   Top companies make meaning, not just money, by paying explicit attention to creating exciting environments in which to work.

6. **Stick to the knitting**
   Business diversity almost never works.

7. **Simple form, lean staff**
   Have a simple structure and outsource a lot.

8. **Simultaneous loose and tight properties**
   A combination of centralised and decentralised gives the best blend: firm central direction and maximum individual autonomy.

There is a lot to take in there. Staying close to customers, valuing staff, giving them responsibility and getting on with things all make eminent sense. But the idea of not diversifying is controversial. Many would point to the number of modern businesses that have thrived precisely because they had the nerve to diversify. Try this for a productivity story: when they turned up the lights at Western Electric's

Hawthorne plant, productivity went up. It went up again when they turned them down. In many companies management is no more than an endless stream of Hawthorne effects, with staff simply reacting to any form of initiative. The views keep coming:

1. **Chronic use of the military metaphor leads people repeatedly to overlook a different kind of organisation**
   This is the machismo we have discussed in previous chapters.

2. **Communication works best when systems are informal and intensity is extraordinary**
   Even better if it is given physical support and there are 'forcing devices', in which case it acts as a tight control system.

3. **The exclusively analytical approach run wild leads to an abstract, heartless philosophy**
   Don't overdo the spreadsheets. Concentrate on character and morale just as much.

4. **Analysing a dead fish does not tell you everything about a live fish**
   Beware paralysis by analysis. Sometimes the thing you are forensically examining tells you nothing about the real world.

5. **Positive reinforcement nudges good things on to the agenda rather than off**
   Successful companies say they don't kill ideas but they do deflect them. This is an important cultural distinction for maintaining morale.

6. **Adhocracy is needed to offset bureaucracy** (Alvin Toffler)

   The best ideas come from random areas, so give people room to breathe.

7. **Small groups are great chunking devices for getting things done**

   Big teams don't work well. *Do it, fix it, try it* is the mantra of experimenting organisations.

The one-sentence summary

A simultaneous blend of loose and tight properties is the perfect blend for running a successful business.

That's a pretty meaty set of ideas to get the chapter rolling. Whatever your view of what it proposes, at the very least all businesspeople should be aware of what the book says, if only so they can adopt a contrary position. One criticism of it is that many of the featured companies have since disappeared. The authors' response is that they weren't writing a book entitled *Forever Excellent*, and that readers can still be inspired by the good things those companies were doing at the time. However, *The Halo Effect* (by Phil Rosenzweig, see later in this chapter) claims that books such as this are little more than storytelling – if it were that easy to follow eight basic principles then all companies would have done so and been a roaring success, which clearly they have not. That's a pretty heavy accusation of the material, so hold that thought because the next author gets it in the neck from Mr Rosenzweig too.

Shattering myths and ensuring long-term success

Built to Last COLLINS & PORRAS
Good to Great JIM COLLINS

In 1994 Jim Collins combined efforts with a guy called Jerry Porras to write *Built to Last*. Although it was not overtly in response to the criticism of *In Search of Excellence* (how come so many of the featured companies have disappeared?), it might as well have been. It conducted a marathon six-year research study to examine companies from their conception, in some cases 100 years before, to their current position, using a comparison company in each case along the way. All had outperformed the stock market by a factor of 15 and were used as the bedrock of a think piece about how companies could create and sustain enduring success. It was a monster that spawned sales over a million, and probably as many boardroom conversations.

In massive detail, it chronicled the successful habits of visionary companies, and generated 12 shattered myths about companies and leadership. None of the following is true, they claim, and there were expansive examples to explain why.

1. **It takes a great idea to start a company**
    No it doesn't. In fact, great ideas brought forward by so-called visionary leaders are found to be negatively correlated with building a successful company.

2. **Visionary companies require great and charismatic visionary leaders**
    Wrong again. Whilst great leadership is always cited as a reason for the success of companies, their

counterparts at other (less successful) companies demonstrate exactly the same qualities of charm, but don't have the same success.

3. The most successful companies exist first and foremost to maximise profits

They don't. They concentrate most on creating the finest company they can, then profits usually follow.

4. Visionary companies share a common subset of 'correct' core values

Not really. In visionary companies, the core values need no rational or external justification, nor do they sway with the trends and fads of the day. In many cases, they are even unique to the company in question.

5. The only constant is change

This rather trite mantra has afflicted many a strategic plan, but actually there can be more value in what stays the same.

6. Blue-chip companies play it safe

No they don't. They simply have far larger reserves of money and people to allow them to experiment. Then if something works, they back it fully, and if it doesn't, they quietly drop it, without jeopardising the health of the mother ship.

7. Visionary companies are great places to work, for everyone

In fact, visionary does not mean soft and undisciplined. They have such a clear idea of who they are that they tend not to have much room for people unsuited to their demanding standards.

8. **Highly successful companies make their best moves by brilliant and complex strategic planning**

   Similar to point six, they are far more likely to try a lot of stuff and keep what works. That's not strategy – it's a high-volume game of reasonably well informed chance.

9. **Companies should hire outside CEOs to stimulate fundamental change**

   With over seventeen hundred years of combined history in visionary companies, the study only found four cases of an outsider coming directly into the role of Chief Executive.

10. **The most successful companies focus primarily on beating the competition**

    As the great sports coaches say, concentrate on what you're going to do, not the other lot.

11. **You can't have your cake and eat it too (the power of AND over OR)**

    Yes you can. Visionary companies do not see things as alternatives. They are able to hold two opposed ideas in the mind at the same time, and sometimes capitalise on both.

12. **Companies become visionary primarily through 'vision statements'**

    Not really. They have an intrinsic sense of their core ideology and have envisioned where they want to reach in the future. Writing it down is almost an afterthought.

What marks out a distinctive business book is a new point of view, and this certainly provided it. All those myths about charismatic leaders, vision statements and complex strategic planning appeared to have been blown out of the water, and this was in the mid-nineties. Much of this thinking remains helpful and relevant, although, given the authority and rigour of the study, it is perhaps surprising that so many companies still don't pay attention to the findings. The clever twist here though is that the book provides lots of alternative thinking to standard corporate behaviour, whilst remaining cunningly disguised in big company clothes.

So if you are interested in providing a counterpoint to stodgy corporate approaches in your company, you will probably find convincing evidence here from a highly respected source that you can cite as evidence to diehard colleagues. The evidence per company is highly detailed, so if you do not know the company (they are all American) or are not interested in it, then you will have to wade through for the bits that support your case. It is also in some respects out of date given recent economic changes, so you need to keep an eye on relevance in that context too.

The one-sentence summary

Ignore charismatic leaders, complex strategies and the competition – if you want enduring success, concentrate on having a common sense of purpose.

By 2001, when Collins published the next big one, *Good to Great,* some things had changed and others hadn't. He had embarked on another mammoth research study (five years this time) to work out how companies can migrate from being merely good to being great. But by the time he had finished, he wondered whether it should in fact have been the prequel to *Built to Last* rather than the sequel. In other words, first you raise your company standards from good to great, and then the resulting organisation will truly be built to last. Strange to conclude then, that perhaps he should have done it the other way round.

So let's have a look at what they found out.

1. Level five leaders build enduring greatness through a paradoxical blend of personal humility and professional will

This would appear to be pretty much the same as point two in *Built to Last*.

2. First who...then what

Get the right people on the bus (and the wrong ones off it), then decide where to drive it.

3. Confront the brutal facts (yet never lose faith)

Work out what you are good at, and do it. Work out what you are bad at, and don't do it.

4. The hedgehog concept

The hedgehog does one thing well (curling into a ball), whilst the fox rushes around, creating the impression of speed. This appears to be the same as sticking to the knitting in *In Search of Excellence*.

5. A culture of discipline

When you have one, you don't need hierarchy. When you have disciplined thought, you don't need bureaucracy.

6. **Technology accelerators**

   These are never the origin of greatness, merely enhancers of it. Good-to-great companies never use technology as the primary means of igniting a transformation.

7. **The flywheel and the doomloop**

   Moves to greatness all happen gradually. Despite the desire of case histories to suggest so, there is no miracle moment.

Also of particular note are the 'dogs that didn't bark' – factors that do *not* play a role in taking a company from good to great, including larger than life celebrity leaders, high executive pay, amazing strategy (all companies claim to have one), mergers and acquisitions, transformation programmes or themes, and being in sexy sectors or industries. None of them apparently make a shred of difference.

The book is also the originator of the BHAG (Big Hairy Audacious Goal), much-loved of testosterone-driven boardrooms the world over. The components parts of this are:

- **what you are deeply passionate about;**

- **what you can be the best in the world at;**

- **what drives your economic engine.**

That's fair enough, but what if you are not hugely passionate about anything commercial, are not that economically driven and can't be the best in the world at something? To be fair, Collins does point out that bad BHAGs are set with bravado and good ones are set with understanding, but they are clearly not for everybody. That's quite enough on this for the moment, because if you read *The Halo Effect* you may decide that the whole study is rubbish. Read on.

A contrary view: all this is no more reliable than storytelling

The Halo Effect PHIL ROSENZWEIG

Don't shoot the messenger. All I can do is report faithfully what Phil Rosenzweig said in his explosive book *The Halo Effect* in 2007. He announced that much of our business thinking is shaped by delusions – errors of logic and flawed judgements that distort our understanding of the real reasons behind a company's performance. These delusions affect the business press and academic research, as well as many bestselling books that promise to reveal the secrets of success or the path to greatness. This is where his analysis of *In Search of Excellence* and *Built to Last* in particular may force you to review your opinion of their findings.

These are serious accusations. According to Rosenzweig, the most pervasive delusion is the Halo Effect. When a company's sales and profits are up, people often conclude that it has a brilliant strategy, a visionary leader, capable employees, and a superb corporate culture. When performance falters, they deduce the opposite but actually little may have changed. In other words, they are attributing success and failure to all the wrong things. If that's true, then the conclusions of most case histories are probably flawed. Other delusions are:

1. Correlation and causality

Two things may be correlated but we may not know which causes which, or whether they are linked at all.

You can show a correlation between the growth in the number of babies and lamp posts in the world, but one did not cause the other.

2. Single explanations

There are usually many reasons for something, not just one. Journalists are particularly guilty of searching desperately for the reason behind various phenomena, when often there simply isn't one.

3. Connecting the winning dots

Finding similar features in successful companies doesn't help because they can't be compared accurately with unsuccessful ones.

4. Rigorous research

If the data aren't good, it doesn't matter how much analysis is done – the conclusions will still be false.

5. Lasting success

This is almost impossible to achieve – almost all high-performing companies regress over time, regardless of what they do. Successful companies also attract a disproportionate amount of interest and study, which usually means they are over-analysed.

6. Absolute performance

Performance is relative, not absolute. A company can improve and fall behind its rivals at the same time. In that respect, it may have done everything brilliantly, but still be deemed to have been lacklustre.

7. Wrong end of the stick

Successful companies may have highly-focused strategies, but that doesn't mean such strategies guarantee success. The same strategy may not work in another company, so attempting to copy them may be pointless.

8. Organisational physics

Performance doesn't obey immutable laws of nature and cannot be predicted with the accuracy of science. Things go up and down anyway, so sometimes success is down to nothing more than luck.

The one-sentence summary
Beware of the wisdom offered by business gurus because it may be little more than false patter and naive arguments that could mislead you.

Nassim Nicholas Taleb, author of *The Black Swan*, described this as 'one of the most important management books of all time.' It is hugely thought-provoking and questions many pieces of received wisdom that so many people in the business world take for granted. So at the very least you might like to look more closely at what you believe to be true from the lessons you thought, up until now, were gospel. The author makes his arguments in an unsparing and direct way that should appeal to a broad audience. Certainly any managers who want to separate fact from fiction should have a look at it. Chances are, armed with the observations in it, you will be able to spot a piece of flawed thinking in your very next document or meeting.

Intuition and action

Making It Happen JOHN HARVEY-JONES

Making It Happen, published in 1988, purported to offer a radical and refreshing business philosophy that would provide a stark contrast to 'the pat solutions and manipulative techniques of so many management books.' John Harvey-Jones claimed that it is possible to run a company with time and respect for everyone involved, and that this approach enables a company to excel. He worked for ICI for 30 years, becoming one of the great management gurus, and ending up with a TV series in which he played the role of troubleshooter in a variety of companies. The book is not a manual or a prescriptive description of the only ways in which things can be done. Instead it is based on his intimate personal experience.

Management is ultimately about people. It is an art, not a science. The artistry lies in the combination of skills, perceptions, intuitions, and combined experiences that are continually different and almost invariably unique. In Harvey-Jones's opinion, there are two types of manager:

1. **The Thoughtful Manager**
   ...who is continually adding to skills and considering changes in the art form.

2. **The Closed Mind Manager**
   ...who attempts continuously to replicate successful solutions in situations which are, almost invariably, totally different.

Naturally, he extols the virtues of the former over the latter. Thoughtful managers regard what they do as an art, whereas those with a closed mind keep reapplying the same formulae to situations that actually require something more subtle. As a result, their off-the-shelf approaches often don't suit the job in hand. Making it happen is the most important part of any idea, and the prime management problem in any company. Crucially, tasks don't get done without the commitment of those who have to execute it. This means that just setting the direction of something often isn't enough – the 'how' of how something will get done needs to be thoroughly worked out as well (see *Execution* in Chapter 6).

The one-sentence summary
Making it happen is the most important part of any idea, and the prime management problem in any company.

Setting the direction is important, but how it is going to get done matters more. The people need to be 'switched on', and ownership of the strategic objective must be transferred to those who are to enact it – the power of good delegation. Ordering people around doesn't work well. This is an important counterpoint to dictatorial management styles, and requires a great deal of sensitivity and effort to enact – not all managers can be bothered to take the time to do this.

Management is about change, and maintaining a high rate of change. Without change nothing is possible. Whether comfortable or not, it is inevitable. The UK has a particular love of the old and a seeming contempt for the new – Harvey-Jones was writing over 20 years ago but does this observation still ring a bell in some companies?

Values and beliefs in a company cannot be created out of thin air. Unless they are real, and permeate everything that is done, they will not have any effect. If they cease to be relevant they must either be abandoned or adapted to be applicable to the future. Without the method or the diagrams, this is a similar point to that made by Jim Collins at the beginning of this chapter. Instead, Harvey-Jones reaches the conclusion intuitively via his years of experience.

Looking at books from this era throws up some interesting opportunities to see if certain predictions have indeed come to pass. For example, he predicted that future organisations would have to adapt to the needs of the individual, rather than the other way round. This would release energies, creativity and imagination of a different order from before. As we look back over the last twenty years or so, this prediction appears to be right.

He also claimed that there is no area of activity in the UK that does not badly need an improvement in managerial skill, which was also probably true. There are no sections, charts or diagrams in the book, so this is more like reading a novel. As such, we cannot claim that his methods have been proven to work, only that the spirit of what he suggested remains as applicable today as it was then.

Alternative views and a twisted future?

The Age of Unreason CHARLES HANDY

A year later, in 1989, Charles Handy wrote *The Age of Unreason*. The world is changing fast, he said, and we need to change with it. The numbers prove it, and companies and governments need to acknowledge this and think differently. The future is not inevitable. We can influence it, if we know what we want it to be.

Discontinuous change requires discontinuous thinking, and that means looking at everything in a new way. Upside down thinking can make you view work as the best of the four-letter words. It doesn't have to be as it currently is. We work for 100,000 hours in our lives, but there are many different ways to divide this up, and it doesn't have to be as formulaic as you might ordinarily think. Here Handy was very much predicting flexi-working in the way that we have come to see it. His calculation was based on 47 (hours a week) x 47 (weeks a year) x 47 (years). This was very much a standard corporate job post-war. A generation later he suggested that his son and daughter could expect their jobs to add up to, on average, 50,000 hours: 37 x 37 x 37.

Modern Portfolio Man has five types of work:

- *Wage work* – **money paid for time given;**

- *Fee work* – **money paid for results delivered;**

- *Home work* – **all the tasks that make a home function;**

- *Gift work* – **work done for free outside home, such as charity work;**

- *Study work* – **training and reading.**

The knack is to analyse all these needs and strike the right blend of activity and income generation. In the past, for most men, their work portfolio only really had one item in it – a risky strategy in any walk of life. He introduced the idea of the Shamrock Organisation – a three part structure containing a core of well-qualified technicians and professionals, the contractual fringe including individuals and organisations and the flexible (part-time) labour force. He was even prescient enough to predict the possibility of a fourth leaf in which the customers do the work for the company, in the same way that co-creators do on the Internet today. Change was Handy's central theme, and it was he who explained that if you put a frog in boiling water it will eventually let itself be boiled to death. Charming, but poignant.

The one-sentence summary
We will not survive unless we actively respond to the radical way our world is changing.

Upside down thinking forces the reader to look at things differently. There are many different types of intelligence, and all have value. He outlines seven:

1. **Analytical intelligence**
   The sort we measure in IQ tests and exams.

2. **Pattern intelligence**
   Musicians, mathematicians and computer programmers who see patterns that others do not.

3. **Musical intelligence**
   This can clearly earn more money than conventional office skills, albeit for fewer people.

4. **Physical intelligence**
   Sportsmen and women are the obvious example.

5. **Practical intelligence**
   This is the sort that enables someone to dismantle a television without being able to name the parts.

6. **Intrapersonal intelligence**

   People who are in tune with others' feelings are very valuable.

7. **Interpersonal intelligence**

   The ability to get on with others.

These are the sorts of characteristics that allow for a broader view of skills and intelligence. He pushes hard against 'endemic group-think', where everyone agrees with each other without thinking properly. This is no way for companies to proceed. In fact, 'work is much more fun than fun', as Noel Coward once said.

The ideas keep coming. Words are heralds of social change; by watching the way language changes, we can spot the linguistic signposts of social change. Negative capability is the ability to make mistakes and learn from them. He rounds the whole thing off on an optimistic note: the Age of Unreason could become the Age of Greatness if people's original goodness could come to the fore. Looking at things differently is to be encouraged and will always lead to better outcomes. This view is as true and fresh now as it was 20 or so years ago, like most of these classics. Notwithstanding Phil Rosenzweig's contrary position, they contain a series of timeless truths that remain relevant today.

CHAPTER 4 WISDOM

- A simultaneous blend of loose and tight properties is the perfect blend for running a successful business.

- Ignore charismatic leaders, complex strategies and the competition – if you want enduring success, concentrate on having a common sense of purpose.

- Beware of the wisdom offered by business gurus because it may be little more than false patter and naive arguments that could mislead you.

- Making it happen is the most important part of any idea, and the prime management problem in any company.

- We will not survive unless we actively respond to the radical way our world is changing.

" That's a 'right brain' concept and sadly we're 'left brainers'. "

CHAPTER 5.
CREATIVITY: CAN YOU LEARN IT?

How different minds work

A Whole New Mind DANIEL H. PINK

Here we try to examine the business angles of creativity, and see whether progress can be made by we humble mortals who may not have a creative streak that comes naturally. *A Whole New Mind* by Daniel H. Pink was published in 2006 and subtitled *Why right-brainers will rule the future*. What does he mean by this?

According to Pink, the age of 'left-brain' dominance is gone. This is represented by practical and logical practitioners such as lawyers, doctors, accountants and engineers (the careers our parents probably wanted us to pursue). Instead, the future belongs to designers, inventors, teachers and storytellers – creative and emphatic 'right-brain' thinkers. He believes that the abilities of right-brain thinkers mark the fault line between who gets ahead and who doesn't. Drawing on research from around the world, he outlines six fundamentally human abilities that are essential for professional success and personal fulfilment, and suggests how it is possible to master them.

The six senses that contribute to this are:

1. **Design**

   Design is a classic whole-minded aptitude – a combination of utility and significance – and we are all now more conscious of it.

2. **Story**

   Stories are more evocative than pure facts – context and emotion are crucial to the ability to remember things.

3. **Symphony**

   This is all about putting everything together. Lots of people can analyse, but how many can synthesise?

4. **Empathy**

   This is the ability to imagine yourself in someone else's position and understand their situation.

5. **Play**

   This is an important component in creativity and relaxation (*The Play Ethic* by Pat Kane is featured in the sister book to this one *Marketing Greatest Hits* A & C Black, 2010).

6. **Meaning**

   This has become a central aspect to our work and lives, and is effectively what every human searches for.

If this all sounds a bit ethereal, it's not supposed to be. Pink explains the context for all this by highlighting three crucial 'A factors': Abundance, Asia and Automation. There is much more of everything now, so almost every market is over-supplied. There are also more people who can do what you do, many of whom come from the East. And if they can't do it, a machine probably can. The upshot of these three phenomena is that we all need to think harder about what we are offering, because if what we offer is ordinary, we will probably face lack of demand or overwhelming competition from other countries or machines.

If this applies to you, you need to be High Concept and High Touch – that means creating things with a high emotional level and understanding the subtleties of human interaction. That's where the six senses come in. At the end of each section describing these, there are a series of exercises and suggestions as to how you can improve your capability in that area. They are too numerous to name in full, so let's take design as an example. Pink suggests that you keep a notebook of all the best pieces of design you come across; channel your annoyance by thinking of appliances that bother you and working out how they can be improved; read more design magazines and go to more museums; choose an object you love, put it on the table and work out why it is so pleasing and choose things in your life that will endure.

The one-sentence summary
We need to create things with a high emotional level and understand the subtleties of human interaction.

There are lots of excellent quotes in the book such as:

'The guy who invented the wheel was an idiot. The guy who invented the other three, he was a genius.' SID CAESAR

'The opposite of play isn't work. It's depression. To play is to act out and be willful, exultant and committed as if one is assured of one's prospects.' BRIAN SUTTON-SMITH

The whole theme of it will suit the new breed of non-conformist free thinkers. In other words, all the artisans and free spirits who have been told for years that they had their head in the clouds can now celebrate the fact that their skills have arguably become more valuable than those of traditional, steady, left-brain thinkers. In truth though, the value lies on the boundary between the two.

Seth Godin (see later this chapter) described it as *'one of those rare books that marks a turning point, one of those books you wish you'd read before everyone else did'*, and Tom Peters called it *'a miracle'*, so it is definitely worth a look.

Suggested methods for encouraging creativity

See Feel Think Do MILLIGAN & SMITH

There has always been a debate about whether creativity should be random or whether it can be subject to any sort of system. That in turn leads to discussion about whether anyone can follow such a system and therefore 'be creative', or whether this remains the domain of intrinsically talented 'creative' people. In 2006, Milligan & Smith wrote *See Feel Think Do,* subtitled *The Power of Instinct in Business.*

Instinct is much more powerful in business than over-reliance on research or data, which can only provide you with a rearview mirror picture, they claim. Certainly, this echoes the point that companies now have too much data, and usually don't know what to do with it. Focus groups and MBA models are not as good as human instinct or a passion to make a difference, they believe. By watching and empathising with real customers and how they act, we can evolve better ideas that solve their real needs, rather than hypothetical ones dreamt up in marketing departments.

See Feel Think Do is a sequence that sums up how these intuitive ideas can come to fruition.

1. See

Experience it for yourself.

What is the current customer experience like? What do they value (or not)? What hassles do they experience? How do we currently differentiate?

2. Feel

Empathise with your customers.

How do I feel about the experience? How do customers and employees feel? What do they like and dislike? What frustrates them?

3. Think

There is no such thing as stupid idea*.

Why do we do it this way? How could it be better? Why can't we do it? Can we turn this into an opportunity?

4. Do

Make it so.

What changes are needed to people, processes, and products? How do we get our people and customers excited about it? How will we know if we are successful?

*This is clearly untrue. There are lots of bad ideas around, so you have to be mindful of this.

The good news is that this is a perfectly sound method that you can apply to any business to see what needs to be changed. Follow the questions and see where it leads you with your current issue. *Why?* is a very powerful question and is not asked often enough in business (see another of my books, *So What?*). There are also scores of case histories to show how it all works (or doesn't): Carphone Warehouse, Apple iPod, Sony, Heinz, Harley Davidson, First Direct, Barclays, Geek Squad, Cathay Pacific, TNT, and many more.

The one-sentence summary
**Instinct is a powerful tool so long as it is
preceded by high quality observation of, and
empathy with, the issue in question.**

In essence, this is probably one of the oldest conceptual models in business, or indeed life. That is to say, observe what someone is experiencing, then use your empathy and intuition, honed by years of experience, to understand the problem and improve something. And whilst the process provides a framework, in this respect it isn't that remarkable. Arguably, good business people should be doing this instinctively anyway. However, there is a catch, and it lies in the phrase 'honed by years of experience'. Those of us who have been around a while may well have this in our armoury. Less experienced colleagues may not. This is compounded by the research effect. As Charles Dunstone of Carphone Warehouse points out, 'most research is generally inconclusive.' All of which means that if you do not have deep experience, or if you rely solely on research, you may have no directional instinct to fall back on.

The only way to overcome this may be to push even harder with the *See Feel Think Do* technique. The sub questions already mentioned go some way to helping, but there's more. When seeing, try using 'soft focus' to soak it all up, but not too scientifically. When feeling, remember you are human too, and don't be afraid to express yourself – it's what normal, 'non-business' people do all the time. When thinking, look at cause and effect, and try adding *'Why not?'* alongside *'Why?'* as a searching question. When doing, get highly specific about nuts and bolts, and be honest if the great new idea isn't working.

So, with the odd caveat, anyone can have a bash at 'being creative'. Almost all great thinkers will tell you that a great idea is no good if it remains just that – an idea. So it is perhaps not surprising that any proposed method always finishes in the execution or doing phase, because without it, nothing happens. We'll look at this more in the final chapter.

Randomness is good too

Purple Cow SETH GODIN
Whatever You Think, Think the Opposite PAUL ARDEN

So much for a system. What about jumping off the deep end and generating ideas in a more haphazard way? *Whatever You Think, Think the Opposite,* said Paul Arden in 2006, but first we'll look at Seth Godin's views in *Purple Cow,* first published in 2003. There is absolutely no point in being just like everybody else, he says. The most successful businesses stand out because they do something different. You, or your business, need to be a Purple Cow – something that is remarkably different from any other product.

The old ways of marketing are dead, and being safe is now too risky. Compromise is the boring slot in any market, and all of them are filled. Old-fashioned mass TV-based marketing doesn't work any more, so your product will only survive in a crowded marketplace if you stop advertising and start innovating. *Otaku* is a Japanese word for something that is more than a hobby but less than an obsession. This causes people to pursue remarkable products to a level that is beyond the reason of most normal people. This kind of passion sits well with brands that do a lot more than just function.

An *Ideavirus* is one that spreads vigorously, similar to the point made by Malcolm Gladwell in *The Tipping Point* (2000). Sneezers are the spreading agents – experts who tell everyone about new products on which they are a perceived authority. This is why so many PR agencies want to 'influence the influencer'.

Purple Cow is short and pithy – you can dip in easily, and there are hundreds of examples to back up Godin's assertions. It effectively goads the reader into looking for remarkable products in their industry and beyond. These are the places where decent, original ideas will come from. There is one exception: boring always leads to failure except when being boring is, in itself, remarkable.

The one-sentence summary
Do the opposite of everyone else and you will be more distinctive.

Whatever You Think, Think the Opposite is a quirky little book that explains the benefits of making bad decisions, why unreason is better than reason and shows how risk is the security in your life (remember Charles Handy in the previous chapter?). It's about having the confidence to roll the dice.

The problem with making sensible decisions is that everyone else is doing the same. They are dull, predictable, and lead you nowhere. Unsafe decisions cause you to think and respond in a way you hadn't thought of. Among the snappy aphorisms Arden offers are:

1. 'I want' is better than 'I wish'

2. **It's better to regret what you have done than what you haven't**

3. **Instead of waiting for perfection, run with what you've got, and fix it as you go**
    Too many people spend too much time trying to perfect something too early.

4. **There is no right point of view**
    There are personal, conventional, large and small ones. You are always both right and wrong. Advances in any field are built upon people with the small or personal point of view.

5. **Steal from anywhere that resonates with inspiration or fuels your imagination**
    Authenticity is invaluable. Originality isn't.

'It's not where you take things from – it's where you take them to.' JEAN-LUC GODARD

What is a good idea anyway? One that happens – as we have already established. One that doesn't, was not a good idea. If an idea is not taken up as a solution to a problem it has no value.

The book is packed full of inspirational and contrary thoughts – just the place to start if you are bogged down or suffering from inertia. Until the Mexico Olympics of 1968, high jumpers faced the bar and the record stood at 5' 8". Dick Fosbury turned his back on it and leapt 7' 4", by thinking the opposite of everyone else. In 1889 George Eastman invented the Kodak brand. It means nothing but was chosen because it was short, was not open to mispronunciation, and could not be associated with anything else.

'The reasonable man adapts himself to the world. The unreasonable man adapts the world to himself. All progress depends on the unreasonable man.' GEORGE BERNARD SHAW

Meetings are for those with not enough to do. They are performances, acts to convince people of their own importance. The world is what you think of it. So think of it differently and your life will change. This book is all about jumping off points, so don't expect to be guided by the hand through the creative process. The overall message is to take a chance and go for it.

Embracing new ideas

Here Comes Everybody CLAY SHIRKY

If you can't generate startling ideas all on your own, don't panic, says Clay Shirky in *Here Comes Everybody* (2008). For the first time we have the tools to make group action a reality and it's going to change the world. We used to do little things for love and big things for money – now we can do big things for love. What does this mean for creativity? It means that you can float a half-baked germ of an idea in the right community and everyone else will help you polish it, or find a better one. And if you choose the right audience, they'll do it for free because they enjoy it. This is something that businesses have only just begun to realise.

The book has a number of main tenets:

- **sharing anchors communities;**

- **everyone is now a media outlet – they can publish, then filter;**

- **personal motivation leads to collaborative production;**

- **collective action creates institutional challenges;**

- **everything is getting faster and faster;**

- **failure now costs nothing (most ideas are bad, but it is now cheaper to at least try something).**

Management challenges grow faster than organisational size, so more is different. Most of the barriers to group action have now collapsed. So have transaction costs, so the original work of Ronald Coase (see *Wikinomics* in Chapter 1) has now been thrown into some confusion. The Birthday Paradox shows that we have a poor grasp of probability. What are the chances of two people in a group of 36 sharing a birthday? You'd think it would be 36 divided by 365 days, yielding one in 10, but there are actually 600 possible pairs of birthdays in a group of 36 (an 80 per cent chance). That's the difference between thinking solely from a personal perspective rather than a group one. At a group level, sending an email is now a kind of publishing, which has the power to bring down companies. On a personal one, (and in answer to those who claim that much of what is on the Internet is unedited rubbish) this material gets posted in public, but is not *for* the public.

The one-sentence summary
If you want a truly interesting creative idea, try asking the audience that cares about it most.

The tragedy of the commons is that, although each shepherd can see that everyone would benefit from restraint (not overgrazing), the odds are against it because the whole arrangement falls apart if just one person is selfish. This problem does not afflict online communities because everyone can afford to fail without penalty. Social awareness has three main levels:

- **when everybody knows something;**

- **when everybody knows that everybody knows;**

- **when everybody knows that everybody knows that everybody knows.**

All of these levels have now been exposed and squashed together by the speed with which ideas can be transmitted on the Internet. This means that the 'fitness landscape' has completely changed. The fitness landscape is a metaphorical area in which, for any problem or goal, there is a vast array of possibilities to explore but only a few valuable spots to discover. Companies tend to stick with the early, obvious ones, and so end up with fairly mediocre ideas, products and solutions. Huge numbers of interested people on the Web can achieve a great deal more, if properly harnessed, as evidenced by Wikipedia.

There are many places from which you can derive creative inspiration. There are probably inspirational people in your company, if you can enthuse them sufficiently. If you can't, try overlaying some element of method (not too much, enough to stimulate and direct). If that doesn't work, try something utterly random, and if that still yields nothing, consider asking the market. You might be surprised by the amount of work they are prepared to put in, and the amount of ingenuity they volunteer.

CHAPTER 5 WISDOM

- We need to create things with a high emotional level and understand the subtleties of human interaction.

- Instinct is a powerful tool as long as it is preceded by high quality observation of, and empathy with, the issue in question.

- Do the opposite of everyone else and you will be more distinctive.

- If you want a truly interesting creative idea, try asking the audience that cares about it most.

"And at that point we thought the hell with it, took our hands off the wheel and went off for a golfing week".

CHAPTER 6.
ORGANISATION:
HOW TO GET ON
WITH IT

Why bother?

Hello Laziness CORINNE MAIER
How to be Idle TOM HODGKINSON

Before we go thundering into how you can rush about all day, be supremely organised and boost your productivity by 100 per cent, let's just pause and consider a seemingly outrageous question: when you are in business, do you really have to be busy? I know it's all the rage to be in meetings until the end of time, but really, might it be possible to be highly effective without tearing around all day? A couple of books shed some fascinating light on the matter, and this is where you'll see that, with the right approach, there is no reason why a number of apparently sociological books can't have a significant bearing on your work life. The purist might not classify some of the books in this chapter as strictly business, but I believe it's important to view your business life in a broader context.

We'll start with a controversial French lady called Corinne Maier, who wrote *Hello Laziness* (originally in French) in 2004. This is a highly unusual book that provides a counterpoint to all those who suggest that increasing productivity is the key to success. She says that you can be a slacker and get away with it and that only by reducing your productivity to zero do you have any chance of climbing the corporate ladder. Hard work and long hours won't get you anywhere. Crikey. That'll have CEOs the world over spitting coffee into their in trays. This lady is so counter-cultural that she was due to be disciplined by her employers for reading a newspaper in a meeting (the action was subsequently dropped).

She pulls no punches and the accusations keep coming

thick and fast. Companies don't care. They hate individuals who don't conform. They talk gibberish, use people as pawns and move them around so no one can keep track. They have no ethics, no culture, and have mastered the art of appearing more intelligent than they actually are. She generates typologies for different types of idiots: Mr Average, The Hollow Man(ager), Consultants who con, Time-wasters, Yes-men, and Nobodies, among others. The idea that business is effectively doomed is an intriguing one. What is a job for, she asks? Many workers genuinely don't know what they are paid for, so why should they fear being lazy?

She then generates 10 new commandments of work, which are:

1. **Salaried work is the new slavery.**

2. **It's pointless trying to change the system.**

3. **The work you do is fundamentally pointless.**

4. **You'll be judged on your ability to conform, not your work.**

5. **Never accept positions of responsibility.**

6. **Seek out the most useless jobs.**

7. **Hide away and stay there.**

8. **Learn how to read the subtle cues that tell you who else has rumbled all this.**

9. **Temporary staff do all the work – treat them well.**

10. **Business ideology is no more 'true' than communism.**

The one-sentence summary
If you want to get promoted, do as little as possible (but be aware that you may also be fired).

It's hard not to like this stuff. Pretty much everyone who has worked in a corporation will recognise the character types, the politics, and the greasy pole of promotion. The tricky bit is to work out whether carrying out what she suggests is a wise thing to do. As well as reflecting many of the novel working practices in corporate France, you need to bear in mind that if you choose to enact a large proportion of this book, you may well get fired.

Compare this stance with that of Tom Hodgkinson in *How to be Idle* (2004). He edits a magazine called *The Idler,* so he should know. As far as he is concerned, society today extols the virtues of efficiency and frowns upon laziness, but as Oscar Wilde once said, 'doing nothing is hard work'. As modern life grows ever more demanding, the loafers of this world may well feel the odds stacking against them, so this book offers an antidote to the work-obsessed culture that puts so many obstacles between us and our dreams. It offers suggestions on how to reclaim your right to sleep in, skive off, lunch at leisure, have a hangover and take time out, and how to let the day slip past you in the best possible way. In doing so, he suggests, you'll be taking back control of your life.

In a narrative form, the book moves through the day from morning to night, and suggests what you can do to enjoy life more, and not be a slave to work, at various times in the day. For example, lying in bed half awake – what sleep researchers call the hypnagogic dream state – is positively beneficial to health and happiness, and can help prepare you mentally for the problems and tasks ahead. It is also the time when some of our best ideas come to us. The rational 'overmind' largely ignores the emotional or spiritual 'under-mind', but this is where we build up the strength to cope with life's struggles. Nobody knows why but sleep can solve many of our problems. Apparently insurmountable problems almost always look better in the morning.

'It is a common experience that a problem difficult at night is resolved in the morning after the committee of sleep has worked on it.' JOHN STEINBECK

In pretty much every business context we feel (or are made to feel?) guilty about taking time off, and we shouldn't. Americans now work an extra month a year compared with 30 years ago, averaging nine hours a day. Life is supposed to be getting easier, but we still elect to overwork. As such, those overdoing it in the workplace would do well to take a little time out and absorb the contents of this book, if only to check whether they lack balance between work and relaxation. This is essentially a charming essay with a series of thoughts about the work/life balance, so strict application to business issues has to be regarded in a philosophical light. There are tonal and lifestyle suggestions throughout, but don't expect a method that will revolutionise your life – it's the spirit of it that counts.

How large companies do it

Execution BOSSIDY & CHARAN

Right. After that philosophical interlude, let's go right to the other end of the spectrum and see how the hard-as-nails big corporations organise things and get them done. It's the bane of their lives: the CEO gets up and announces an amazing initiative, and a year later nothing has happened. *Execution*, by Bossidy & Charan (2002), grapples with this very problem.

Subtitled *The Discipline of Getting Things Done*, it explains how leaders of big companies can get people to deliver what they say they will. It's no good formulating a 'vision' and leaving others to get on with it – bosses need to be passionately and deeply engaged, and must have robust dialogue about people, strategy and operations all the time. People mistakenly think of execution as the tactical side of the business, which seduces leaders into concentrating on the so-called bigger issues. This leads to a gap between the promises leaders make and the results the organisation delivers. To show how much of a problem this is in big companies; in 2000, 40 of the top Fortune 200 company CEOs were removed for that very reason. To truly understand execution, you need to understand that:

- **execution is a discipline and integral to strategy;**

- **execution is the major job of the business leader;**

- **execution must be a core element of a company's culture.**

It is also, of course, a systematic way of exposing reality and acting on it. This is a theme we have returned to time and again. It is pointless having apparently wonderful ideas in an ivory tower if none of them are enacted, and you cannot always take it on faith that someone else will carry them out for you, even if they have said that they will. According to Bossidy and Charan, leaders need to engage in seven essential behaviours to be good at execution:

1. **Know your people and your business**
   In companies that don't execute, the leaders are usually out of touch with the day-to-day realities.

2. **Insist on realism**
   People try to avoid reality because it makes them uncomfortable – even leaders.

3. **Set clear goals and priorities**
   People only execute well when they have one or two clear things to do.

4. **Follow through**
   People need to be held accountable for something happening, otherwise it won't.

5. **Reward the doers**
   Most companies do a poor job of linking rewards to true performance.

6. **Expand people's capabilities through coaching**
   'Give a man a fish and you'll feed him for a day; teach a man how to fish, and you'll feed him for a lifetime.'

7. **Know yourself**
   See the qualities needed in the next section.

The one-sentence summary
Concentrate on getting something done as much as having the original idea.

As you would hope, there is much common sense here about execution. A leader who says: 'I've got ten priorities' doesn't know what he's talking about. Leaders have to have emotional fortitude, which is made up of authenticity, self-awareness, self-mastery and humility. We don't think our way into a new way of acting, we act our way into a new way of thinking. The social software of execution is the people. Meetings without robust debate mean that people don't state their misgivings, so nothing is enacted and leaders get the behaviour they exhibit and tolerate. If a strategy does not address the 'hows', it is destined for failure. The crucial question is: can the business execute the strategy? All of these points could prove to be a timely wake-up call for those senior executives in large corporations who have spent too much time 'strategising' and not enough time actually getting their hands dirty with action.

How small companies do it

Why Entrepreneurs Should Eat Bananas, SIMON TUPMAN

Another way of viewing an organisation is to look at the individuals within it. And what better place to scrutinise them than through the eyes of someone who runs their own business? *Why Entrepreneurs Should Eat Bananas* by Simon Tupman (2006) does just that. It has 101 inspirational ideas for growing your business and yourself. Take positive control of your life, he says – don't let circumstances rule you.

The three Ps are *professional skills, purpose,* and *passion.* You need to be able to tick all three to claim that you are happy in life and work. If not, you need to make some changes. There are three types of people in the world: those who make things happen, those who watch things happen, and those who wonder what happened. You need to see the world for what it is, examine best practice, connect with existing customers, find new ones, connect with your people (if you have them), and then connect with life itself. Enthusiasm comes from the Greek *en theos* ('inner God'), and you need lots of it.

'Nothing great was ever achieved without enthusiasm.' RALPH WALDO EMERSON

So if you are working long and exhausting hours, busting a gut over unprofitable customers, reluctant to delegate, lacking in self-confidence, suffering unhealthy stress levels or not devoting enough time to family and friends, try some of these ideas:

1. **Start leading or consider leaving**
   Negative people need to move on.

2. **Leave the office no later than 5.30**
   It's amazing what you can achieve if you do.

3. **Understand your value**
   Too many people undervalue themselves.

4. **Keep on moving**
   This is a health point: the more you move, the healthier you are.

5. **Develop a 'spoken logo'**
   This is your elevator pitch that goes beyond the factual and into the emotional benefit of what you do.

The one-sentence summary
Whatever type of place you work in, you need to take an entrepreneurial view of your work.

The title of this book is in fact a misnomer. It is meant to catch your attention and the answer to it is simply that bananas are good for you, which is a bit of a letdown. Nor is it specifically about entrepreneurs – it is to do with anyone who works in a company and the attitude they need to adopt in order to succeed. As well as having over a hundred ideas from which you can choose, there are lots of different forms in the appendix, such as customer surveys, self-assessments, and team performance questionnaires that you can use straightaway to analyse your position. The main message is clear: even if you work in a large, sluggish corporation, you can increase your happiness and success by behaving as though you were running your own business and by acting in a more sprightly manner than everyone else.

How you can do it

How to Get More Done FERGUS O'CONNELL
Getting Things Done DAVID ALLEN
Many of us feel we are struggling against an endless stream of tasks each day – both in our work and our personal lives. *How To Get More Done* by Fergus O'Connell (2008) claims to give you everything you need to get things under control in one week. Some would call that a tall order, but that's what he claims. You need to embrace three new behaviours:

- **not doing stuff;**

- **only doing the right stuff;**

- **doing as little as possible when doing the right stuff.**

Don't do the small things – do the ones that are big in relation to how important they are to your life. You need a system, but it must be flexible. It must include a list, a way of tracking appointments, a filing system and a way of recording where your time goes. To work out how to reprogram yourself, you need to understand Dilts's Neurological Levels of Change, which are (in order of importance):

1. **Identity**
   Who are you? This is your core sense of self and your mission in life.

2. **Beliefs and values**
   Why am I doing this? (This can be both enabling and limiting).

3. **Capabilities**
   How do I deal with things? What are the skills and strategies that you use?

4. **Behaviour**
   Specific actions and reactions in your daily environment.

5. **Environment**
   The external context in which you operate.

If you want to change your approach, you'll have to knuckle down and fill out the whole system to get a result. You need to figure out everything you have to do, pick a time period, list all your projects, add functional things like meetings and reports, allow for interruptions and map it all out. Now work out how much time it will take to do it all. Write a dance card that shows what it all adds to – you may discover that it is twice the time you actually have. Now you can set about doing something about it. For example, there are lots of ways to say no to people: question why it needs to be done, deflect some requests, delegate more, negotiate, challenge demands for your time, make people aware of the consequences and so on.

You need to become adept at deploying these techniques, and dealing with your guilt by stopping the sources of it and building up your resistance. When planning a task, say 'I'll have a look at it,' work out what you have been asked to do and the sequence for getting it done, decide who will do what, allow for the unexpected, go back to the asker and say: 'Here's what I can do.' In short, you need to let more stuff 'go hang'.

The one-sentence summary
Do fewer things, only do the right things, and take less time doing them.

David Allen concurs with a fair chunk of this in *Getting Things Done* (2001). He believes that it is perfectly possible for a person to have an overwhelming number of things to do and still function productively with a clear head and a positive sense of relaxed control. Among his suggestions are:

- **have one filing system;**

- **turn your in tray upside down and work on the principle of First In First Out (FIFO), not Last In First Out (LIFO) as many people do;**

- **use a five-stage system: collect, process, organise, review, do;**

- **do it, delegate it, or defer it;**

- **nothing should take more than two minutes, nor should it go back into your in tray.**

It's worth noting that the two authors in this section are at odds on this last point. O'Connell believes that the two-minute rule only allows you to get the small things done, when in fact you should only be doing the big things. He doesn't mean with regard to how long they will take, but how important they are to you. Back to Allen: he says that the four crucial factors are context, time, energy and priority. We should all be able to review our tasks in relation to these four factors, sort through them and get them done effectively. There is also a six-level model for reviewing your work, using an aerospace analogy:

50,000+ feet: life

40,000 feet: three- to five-year vision

30,000 feet: one- to two-year goals

20,000 feet: areas of responsibility

10,000 feet: current projects

Runway: current actions

If you have problems with organisation and getting things done, this book could certainly sort you out. The more relaxed you are, the more effective you will be (as in karate).

Applied to all parts of your life, and not necessarily the most urgent bits, this becomes Black Belt Management. The key to being relentlessly effective is to concentrate only on the very next physical action required to move the situation forward. There are lots of good inspirational quotes:

'This constant preoccupation with all the things we have to do is the single largest consumer of time and energy.'

'Blessed are the flexible, for they shall not be bent out of shape.'

'Everything should be made as simple as possible, but not simpler.'

'I am rather like a mosquito in a nudist camp. I know what I want to do, but I don't know where to begin.'

'The middle of every project looks like a disaster.'

'Talk does not cook rice.'

'There are risks and costs to a program of action, but they are far less than the long-range costs of comfortable inaction.'

If you need even more on how to get stuff done, do look at another of my books, *Tick Achieve.*

Getting your attitude right

S.U.M.O. PAUL MCGEE

And so we reach the end of our journey. Being a review of other people's wisdom, this was not so much a sequential run as a set of informed groupings of helpful material. As we have reviewed the issues that confront businesses, we have also had to entertain opposing views simultaneously – arguably the art of real intelligence. So we will finish off with the one thing that binds it all together, or ruins everything: your attitude. You could absorb every gem in this book and still be useless at work if you haven't got your head straight.

Paul McGee wrote *S.U.M.O.* in 2006. It stands for Shut Up, Move On, and is subtitled *The Straight-Talking Guide to Creating and Enjoying a Brilliant Life*. We all long for success and enjoyment but unfortunately we don't always get either of them. Have you ever thought that it might be your own attitude that is holding you back?

The way you think is a major factor in determining how your life unfolds. The book argues that by taking responsibility for your life, you can fulfil your potential, seize opportunities, enjoy relationships, succeed at work and respond to adverse situations with a positive attitude. You are encouraged to take an honest look at your life, remembering that it is never too late to change. We can all dump the victim t-shirt, develop 'fruitier' thinking and ditch the idea that whatever will be will be (McGee calls this *Ditching Doris Day,* after the song *Que Sera*). When you wear the victim t-shirt you become a passenger in life and allow circumstances and other people to determine your direction. As this has become more prevalent, some people have become so aware of their rights that they fail to acknowledge their responsibilities.

This is heavyweight life coaching with a soft centre. There are seven questions to help you *S.U.M.O.*:

1. **Where is this issue on a scale of one to 10?**
   Decide what's really important.

2. **How important will this be in six months' time?**
   Get things in perspective.

3. **Is my response appropriate and effective?**
   Choose your response carefully.

4. **How can I influence or improve the situation?**
   Bring about change.

5. **What can I learn from this?**
   Look for learning in everything.

6. **What will I do differently next time?**
   Learning brings change.

7. **What can I find that's positive in this situation?**
   Open your mind to new possibilities.

The one-sentence summary
**The best way to get something done is to
ignore what's happened before and move on.**

The way you think is influenced by your background, previous experiences, the company you keep and the media. Faulty thinking includes being a persistent inner critic, becoming a broken record, using the martyr syndrome (when I punish me I am actually trying to punish you), and trivial pursuits (what you focus on magnifies). Hippo Time (having a brief wallow) is okay, so long as you snap out of it fairly rapidly and get on to the next thing with a renewed, positive attitude. One thing above all is clear: you will not be a success in business if you have not reconciled what you do at work with your personal life, so you have to get things in perspective.

I hope you have enjoyed our ramble through the best of what business writers can offer. Choose the bits you like most, and give it a go.

CHAPTER 6 WISDOM

- **If you want to get promoted, do as little as possible (but be aware that you may also be fired).**

- **Concentrate on getting something done as much as having the original idea.**

- **Whatever type of place you work in, you need to take an entrepreneurial view of your work.**

- **Do fewer things, only do the right things and take less time doing them.**

- **The best way to get something done is to ignore what's happened before and move on.**

APPENDIX I:
A NEW BUSINESS MANIFESTO

30 points that might help your business

THE BIG THEMES

- Don't fool yourself: much business performance is down to chance, not skill.

- Ignore the experts, stop trying to predict everything, and embrace uncertainty.

- Context is absolutely crucial: what appears to be the cause of something is rarely the real reason it's happening.

- People will make irrational decisions if left to their own devices.

- The Internet has effectively flattened the world to the point where businesses can view the entire thing as both a potential resource and a market.

- The Internet has changed everything, so you need to open up your business to your customers.

BUSINESS STRATEGY

- Concentrate on what you are going to do and don't become obsessed with the competition.

- Customers who are prepared to recommend your product or service are the ultimate barometer of success.

- The Internet has turned traditional economics upside down by making many things free, so look carefully at your reputation and the time you demand from your customers.

- Discipline your business thinking, and the way in which you organise information.

- Treat information with great suspicion until you know the real story.

- Every human being, no matter how diverse, complies with economic logic.

LEADERSHIP

- To be a good leader you have to earn respect.

- Smart leaders set a course, assume it will change, and try to get lots of people to show leadership qualities.

- Successful leaders will take on risk, change and ambiguity.

- If in doubt, trust everyone and do nothing.

- People will always tell you it can't be done, but if you have faith in yourself, it almost always can.

THE CLASSICS

- A simultaneous blend of loose and tight properties is the perfect blend for running a successful business.

- Ignore charismatic leaders, complex strategies and the competition – if you want enduring success, concentrate on having a common sense of purpose.

- Beware of the wisdom offered by business gurus because it may be little more than false patter and naive arguments that could mislead you.

- Making it happen is the most important part of any idea, and the prime management problem in any company.

- We will not survive unless we actively respond to the radical way our world is changing.

CREATIVITY

- We need to create things with a high emotional level and understand the subtleties of human interaction.

- Instinct is a powerful tool as long as it is preceded by high quality observation of, and empathy with, the issue in question.

- Do the opposite of everyone else and you will be more distinctive.

- If you want a truly interesting creative idea, try asking the audience that cares about it most.

ORGANISATION

- If you want to get promoted, do as little as possible (but be aware that you may also be fired).

- Concentrate on getting something done as much as having the original idea.

- Whatever type of place you work in, you need to take an entrepreneurial view of your work.

- Do fewer things, only do the right things, and take less time doing them.

- The best way to get something done is to ignore what's happened before and move on.

APPENDIX II:
THE ONE-MINUTE
SUMMARIES

A Whole New Mind DANIEL H. PINK

WHAT THE BOOK SAYS

- The book is subtitled *Why Right-Brainers Will Rule the Future*.
- The age of 'left-brain' dominance is gone (this is represented by practical and logical practitioners such as lawyers, doctors, accountants and engineers).
- The future belongs to designers, inventors, teachers and storytellers – creative and emphatic 'right-brain' thinkers.
- Abundance, Asia and Automation: there are more people who can do what you do, many come from the East and if they can't do it, a machine probably can, so we all need to think harder about what we are offering.
- If this applies to you, you need to be High Concept and High Touch – that means creating things with a high emotional level and understanding the subtleties of human interaction.
- The six senses that contribute to this are: *design* (we are all more conscious of it – a combination of utility and significance), *story* (stories are more evocative than pure facts – context and emotion are crucial), *symphony* (putting everything together), *empathy* (understanding someone else's situation), *play* (an important component in creativity and relaxation) and *meaning* (what every human searches for).

WHAT'S GOOD ABOUT IT

- There are lots of excellent quotes such as:

'The guy who invented the wheel was an idiot. The guy who invented the other three, he was a genius.' SID CAESAR

'The opposite of play isn't work. It's depression. To play is to act out and be wilful, exultant and committed as if one is assured of one's prospects.' BRIAN SUTTON-SMITH

- At the end of each section there is a series of exercises and suggestions as to how you can improve your capability in that area.
- The whole theme will suit the new breed of non-conformist free thinkers.

WHAT YOU HAVE TO WATCH
- Not much. It's a good read.
- The book is praised by Thomas Friedman (*The World is Flat*) and Seth Godin (*Purple Cow*).

Built To Last COLLINS & PORRAS

WHAT THE BOOK SAYS
- This is the 1994 classic about the successful habits of visionary companies.
- It uses a six-year research study to examine companies from their conception – in some cases 100 years ago – to their current position, using a comparison company in each case along the way. All have outperformed the stock market by a factor of fifteen.
- There are 12 shattered myths about companies and leadership:
    1. It takes a great idea to start a company.
    2. Visionary companies require great and charismatic visionary leaders.
    3. The most successful companies exist first and foremost to maximise profits.
    4. Visionary companies share a common subset of 'correct' core values.
    5. The only constant is change.
    6. Blue chip companies play it safe.
    7. Visionary companies are great places to work, for everyone.

8.   Highly successful companies make their best moves by brilliant and complex strategic planning.
9.   Companies should hire outside CEOs to stimulate fundamental change.
10.   The most successful companies focus primarily on beating the competition.
11.   You can't have your cake and eat it too (the power of AND over OR).
12.   Companies become visionary primarily through 'vision statements'.

None of these is true and the examples explain why.

WHAT'S GOOD ABOUT IT
- Although this book has taken on revered status, much of it remains helpful and relevant.
- Given the authority and rigour of the study, it is perhaps surprising that so many companies still don't pay attention to its findings.
- If you are interested in providing a counterpoint to stodgy corporate approaches, you will probably find convincing evidence here from a respected source.

WHAT YOU HAVE TO WATCH
- It is in some respects out of date given recent economic changes.
- The evidence per company is highly detailed, so if you do not know the company (they are all American) or are not interested in it, then you have to wade through for the bits you want.
- If you read, and agree with, *The Halo Effect*, you may think the whole study is rubbish.

Execution BOSSIDY & CHARAN

WHAT THE BOOK SAYS
- Subtitled *The Discipline of Getting Things Done*, it explains how leaders of big companies can get people to deliver what they say they will.
- It's no good formulating a vision and leaving others to get on with it – bosses need to be passionately and deeply engaged and must have robust dialogue about people, strategy and operations.
- People mistakenly think of execution as the tactical side of the business, which seduces leaders into concentrating on the so-called bigger issues leading to a gap between the promises leaders make and the results the organisation delivers. In 2000, 40 of the top Fortune 200 company CEOs were removed for that very reason.
- To understand execution, you need to understand:
  - ☐ execution is a discipline, and integral to strategy;
  - ☐ execution is the major job of the business leader;
  - ☐ execution must be a core element of a company's culture.
- Execution is also a systematic way of exposing reality and acting on it.

WHAT'S GOOD ABOUT IT
- Leaders need to engage in seven essential behaviours to be good at execution:
  - ☐ know your people and your business;
  - ☐ insist on realism;
  - ☐ set clear goals and priorities;
  - ☐ follow through;
  - ☐ reward the doers;
  - ☐ expand people's capabilities;
  - ☐ know yourself.

- A leader who says: 'I've got ten priorities' doesn't know what he's talking about.
- Leaders have to have emotional fortitude, which is made up of authenticity, self-awareness, self-mastery and humility.
- We don't think our way into a new way of acting, we act our way into a new way of thinking.
- The social software of execution is the people. Meetings without robust debate means that people don't state their misgivings, so nothing is enacted.
- Leaders get the behaviour they exhibit and tolerate.
- If a strategy does not address the 'hows', it is destined for failure.
- The crucial question is: can the business execute the strategy?

WHAT YOU HAVE TO WATCH
- Most of the examples are American, and the book came out in 2002.

Fooled By Randomness NASSIM NICHOLAS TALEB

WHAT THE BOOK SAYS
- Everyone wants to succeed, but what causes some people to be more successful than others? Is it really down to skill and strategy, or something altogether more unpredictable?
- The book is all about how we perceive 'luck' in our personal and professional lives. We often hear that an entrepreneur has 'vision' or that a trader is 'talented' but all too often their performance is down to chance, not skill.

- We fail to understand probability and so continue to believe events are non-random, finding reasons where none exist.
- Black Swans are unexpected random events. This is based on John Stuart Mill's observation that no amount of observations of white swans can prove that all swans are white – the sighting of a single black swan can disprove it. Seeing George Bush alive many times does not prove that he is immortal.
- Many rich people are just lucky idiots.

WHAT'S GOOD ABOUT IT

- This is not a textbook, but there are many thought-provoking messages in it.
- Journalists are bred to not understand randomness – they must have a reason.
- The noise in markets usually disguises the signal.
- Because a rich person can lose it all, they cannot be said to be truly happy until their life is finished (this observtion was made by the Greek legislator Solon, when unimpressed with Croesus, supposedly the richest person ever).
- The Monte Carlo Simulator is a computer program that simulates random occurrences, rather like extended Russian roulette. Examining its behaviour makes nonsense of most so-called patterns in market analysis.
- Those predicting events usually don't know what they are talking about, or what can sensibly be deduced from the data they have.
- There is usually no link between the most recent event and the one about to happen – this is crucial when analysing trends

WHAT YOU HAVE TO WATCH

- The book is quite long and highly technical – it is not for the faint-hearted, despite having sold huge numbers and being translated into 18 languages.
- The author quite enjoys being obscure or obtuse.

Freakonomics LEVITT & DUBNER

WHAT THE BOOK SAYS

- An economist and an inquisitive journalist explore the hidden side of everything.
- They find links and patterns in all sorts of strange areas by asking unconventional questions such as:
  - □ What do estate agents and the Ku Klux Klan have in common?
  - □ Why do drug dealers live with their mothers?
  - □ How can your name affect how well you do in life?
- By using information about the world around us we can get to the heart of what is really going on.
- We need to be much more inquisitive and not accept received wisdom.

WHAT'S GOOD ABOUT IT

- If you follow the thinking behind the whole book, you will never take anything for granted again.
- What appears to be a reason for something rarely is – instead it is often a twisted piece of received wisdom that everyone blindly accepts. Take an example: parents prevent a child from going to play in a house where a gun is owned, but allow them to visit another friend who has a swimming pool. In fact the odds are 1:11,000 of drowning and 1:1 million of gun death.
- We are all terrible risk assessors, and as a result, we often make very dim decisions which fly in the face of the facts.

- There is a massive difference between correlation (two things appear to be linked) and causality (one actually causes the other). We need to distinguish between the two to make sensible decisions.

WHAT YOU HAVE TO WATCH
- In the broadest sense, the book has nothing to do with business.
- However, the enlightened mind can take the principles and apply them to the discernment of truly relevant data, and the kind of inquisitiveness that is essential for any successful strategy.

Free CHRIS ANDERSON

WHAT THE BOOK SAYS
- Old economic certainties are being undermined by a growing flood of free goods because production and distribution costs in many sectors have plummeted to unthinkable levels.
- The flexibility of the online world allows producers to trade ever more creatively, offering items for free to make real or perceived gains elsewhere.
- As an increasing number of things becomes freely available, our decisions to make use of them are determined by the popular reputation of what's on offer and the time we have available for it.
- In the future when we talk of the money economy, we will really be talking about the reputation and time economy.
- The loss leader concept is giving away one thing to get another: the Internet has taken this to a new level.
- The economics of atoms is based on tangible items. The economics of bits is based on storage space and is intangible, leading to 'freeconomics'.

- There are three prices: something, nothing (free) and less than nothing – this is negative price, where you get paid to use a product. There is a gym in Denmark where you pay nothing as long as you go at least once a week.

WHAT'S GOOD ABOUT IT

- Compare with Seth Godin's *Unleashing the Ideavirus*: 20 years ago the top 100 companies either dug something out of the ground or turned a natural resource into something you could hold. Now this applies to only 32 – the others sell ideas.
- The demand you get at a price of zero is many times higher than at a very low price – the 'penny gap' identified by Kopelman.
- Modern business models should:
  - □ build a community around free information;
  - □ use it to design something that people want;
  - □ let those with more money buy more polished versions of the product;
  - □ keep repeating the process.
- The idea of a learning curve was invented by Ebbinghaus in the 19th century to describe improvements when people memorised tasks over many repetitions.
- Information wants to be free:
  - □ access to computers should be unlimited;
  - □ all information should be free;
  - □ mistrust authority;
  - □ computers can change your life for the better.
- Ten principles of Abundance Thinking:
  1. If it's digital, sooner or later it's going to be Free;
  2. Atoms would like to be Free too;
  3. You can't stop Free;
  4. You can make money from Free;
  5. Redefine your market;
  6. Round down;

7. Sooner or later you will compete with Free;
8. Embrace waste;
9. Free makes other things more valuable;
10. Manage for abundance, not scarcity.

WHAT YOU HAVE TO WATCH
- Not much. There is much to ponder here about modern markets.

Getting Things Done DAVID ALLEN

WHAT THE BOOK SAYS
- It is possible for a person to have an overwhelming number of things to do and still function productively with a clear head and a positive sense of relaxed control.
- You should only have one filing system.
- You should turn your in tray upside down and work on the principle of First In First Out (FIFO), not Last In First Out (LIFO) as many people do.
- It's a five-stage system: collect, process, organise, review, do
- Do it, delegate it, or defer it.
- Nothing should take more than two minutes. Nor should you put anything back into your in tray.
- The four crucial factors are context, time, energy and priority.
- There is a six-level model for reviewing your work, using an aerospace analogy: 50,000+ feet: life; 40,000 feet: three- to five-year vision; 30,000 feet: one- to two-year goals; 20,000 feet: areas of responsibility; 10,000 feet: current projects; Runway: current actions.

WHAT'S GOOD ABOUT IT
- If you have problems being organised and getting things done, this book will sort you out.
- The more relaxed you are, the more effective you will be.
- You have to concentrate on the very next physical action required to move the situation forward. There are lots of good quotes:

'This constant preoccupation with all the things we have to do is the single largest consumer of time and energy.'

'Blessed are the flexible, for they shall not be bent out of shape.'

'Everything should be made as simple as possible, but not simpler.'

'I am rather like a mosquito in a nudist camp. I know what I want to do, but I don't know where to begin.'

'The middle of every project looks like a disaster.'

'Talk does not cook rice.'

'There are risks and costs to a program of action, but they are far less than the long-range costs of comfortable inaction.'

WHAT YOU HAVE TO WATCH
- Nothing. This is an international bestseller and it works.

Good to Great JIM COLLINS

WHAT THE BOOK SAYS
- It is the sequel to the 1994 classic about the successful habits of companies.

- It uses a five-year research study to work out how companies can migrate from being merely good to being great. By the time the author had finished, he wondered whether it should in fact have been the prequel.
- 'Level five' leaders build enduring greatness through a paradoxical blend of personal humility and professional will.
- Of particular note are the 'dogs that didn't bark', factors that do *not* play a role in taking a company from good to great, including:
  - □ larger than life celebrity leaders;
  - □ high executive pay;
  - □ strategy (all companies claim to have one);
  - □ technology (it can only accelerate change, not instigate it);
  - □ mergers and acquisitions;
  - □ transformation programmes or themes;
  - □ sexy sectors or industries.

WHAT'S GOOD ABOUT IT
- Although this book has taken on revered status, much of it remains helpful and relevant. You can try to apply the principles:
  - □ *First who...then what*. Get the right people on the bus, then decide where to drive it.
  - □ *Confront the brutal facts (yet never lose faith)*. Work out what you are good at, and do it. Work out what you are bad at, and don't do it.
  - □ *The hedgehog concept*. The hedgehog does one thing well (curling into a ball) whilst the fox rushes around, creating the impression of speed.
  - □ *Culture of discipline*. When you have one, you don't need hierarchy.
  - □ *Technology accelerators*. These are never the origin of greatness, merely enhancers of it.

□ *The flywheel and the doomloop*. All moves to greatness happen gradually – there is no miracle moment.

WHAT YOU HAVE TO WATCH
- The evidence per company is highly detailed, so if you do not know the company (they are all American) or are not interested in it, then you have to wade through for the bits you want.
- If you read, and agree with, *The Halo Effect*, you may think the whole study is rubbish.

Hello Laziness CORINNE MAIER

WHAT THE BOOK SAYS
- This is an unusual book that provides a counterpoint to all those that suggest that increasing productivity is the key to success.
- It says that you can be a slacker and get away with it, and that only by reducing your productivity to zero do you have any chance of climbing the corporate ladder.
- Hard work and long hours won't get you anywhere.
- Companies don't care. They hate individuals who don't conform.
- They talk gibberish, use people as pawns, and move them around so no one can keep track.
- They have no ethics, no culture, and have mastered the art of appearing more intelligent than they actually are.

WHAT'S GOOD ABOUT IT
- It's good to take the opposite view from time to time, if only to test what you believe
- There are typologies of idiots: Mr Average, The Hollow Man(ager), Consultants who con, Time-wasters, Yes-men, and Nobodies

- The idea that business is effectively doomed is an intriguing one
- What is a job for? Many workers genuinely don't know what they are paid for, so why should they fear being lazy?
- The author's 10 new commandments of work are:
  1. Salaried work is the new slavery.
  2. It's pointless trying to change the system.
  3. The work you do is fundamentally pointless.
  4. You'll be judged on your ability to conform, not your work.
  5. Never accept positions of responsibility.
  6. Seek out the most useless jobs.
  7. Hide away and stay there.
  8. Learn how to read the subtle cues that tell you who else has rumbled all this.
  9. Temporary staff do all the work – treat them well.
  10. Business ideology is no more 'true' than communism.

WHAT YOU HAVE TO WATCH

- It is translated from the French and reflects many of the strange working practices in corporate France.
- If you choose to enact a large proportion of this book, you may get fired.

Here Comes Everybody CLAY SHIRKY

WHAT THE BOOK SAYS

- For the first time we have the tools to make group action a reality and it's going to change the world. The book has a number of main tenets:
  - ☐ Sharing anchors communities.
  - ☐ Everyone is now a media outlet – they can publish, then filter.
  - ☐ Personal motivation leads to collaborative production.

- ☐ Collective action creates institutional challenges.
- ☐ Everything is getting faster and faster.
- ☐ Failure now costs nothing (most ideas are bad, but it is now cheaper to at least try something).
- ☐ Management challenges grow faster than organisational size, so more is different.
- ☐ Sending an email is now a kind of publishing, which has the power to bring down companies.
- ☐ In answer to those who claim that much on the Internet is unedited rubbish, much of what gets posted is in public, but not *for* the public.
- ☐ We used to do little things for love, and big things for money – now we can do big things for love.

WHAT'S GOOD ABOUT IT

- The Birthday Paradox shows that we have a poor grasp of probability. What are the chances of two people in a group of 36 sharing a birthday? You'd think it would be 36 divided by 365 days, yielding one in 10, but there are actually 600 possible pairs of birthdays in a group of 36 (an 80 per cent chance).
- Most of the barriers to group action have now collapsed. So have transaction costs, which throws the original work of Ronald Coase (see Wikinomics) into confusion.
- The tragedy of the commons is where each shepherd can see that all would benefit from restraint (not overgrazing) but the odds are against it because the whole arrangement falls apart if just one person is selfish.
- Social awareness has three levels:
  - ☐ When everybody knows something.
  - ☐ When everybody knows that everybody knows.
  - ☐ When everybody knows that everybody knows that everybody knows.
- The fitness landscape is a metaphorical area in which, for any problem or goal, there is a vast array of possibilities to

explore but only a few valuable spots to discover. Companies tend to stick with the early, obvious ones.

WHAT YOU HAVE TO WATCH
- It is fairly long and detailed so you have to dig hard for the nuggets.
- Much of the material echoes the contents of Wikinomics.

How to be Idle TOM HODGKINSON

WHAT THE BOOK SAYS
- Society today extols the virtues of efficiency and frowns upon laziness, but as Oscar Wilde once said: 'doing nothing is hard work'.
- As modern life grows ever more demanding, the loafers of this world may feel the odds stacking against them.
- The book offers an antidote to the work-obsessed culture that puts so many obstacles between ourselves and our dreams. It offers suggestions on how to reclaim your right to sleep in, skive off, lunch at leisure, have a hangover and take time out; and how to let the day slip past you in the best possible way.
- In doing so, you'll be taking control of your life.

WHAT'S GOOD ABOUT IT
- In a narrative form, the book moves through the day from morning to night, and suggests what you can do to enjoy life more and not be a slave to work.
- Lying in bed half awake – what sleep researchers call the hypnagogic dream state – is positively beneficial to health and happiness, and can help prepare you mentally for the problems and tasks ahead. It is also the time when some of our best ideas come to us.

- The rational overmind largely ignores the emotional or spiritual undermind, but this is where we build up strength to cope with life's struggles.
- Nobody knows why but sleep can solve many of our problems. Apparently insurmountable problems look better in the morning.
- We feel guilty taking time off, and we shouldn't. Americans now work an extra month a year compared with 30 years ago, averaging nine hours a day. Life is supposed to be getting easier, but we still elect to overwork.
- Those overdoing it in the workplace would do well to take a little time out and absorb the contents of this book.

WHAT YOU HAVE TO WATCH
- This is a relaxed essay with a series of thoughts about the work/life balance, so strict application to business issues has to be regarded in a philosophical light. There are tonal and lifestyle suggestions throughout, but don't expect a method that will revolutionise your life – it's the spirit of it that counts.

How to Get More Done FERGUS O'CONNELL

WHAT THE BOOK SAYS
- Many of us feel we are struggling against an endless stream of tasks each day – both in our work and our personal lives. This book gives you everything you need to get things under control in one week.
- You need to embrace three new behaviours: not doing stuff; only doing the right stuff; and doing as little as possible when doing the right stuff.
- Don't do the small things – do the things that are big in relation to how important they are to your life.

- You need a system, but it must be flexible.
- It must include a list, a way of tracking appointments, a filing system and a way of recording where your time goes.
- To work out how to reprogram yourself, you need to understand Dilts's Neurological Levels of Change, which are (in order of importance):
  - □ *Identity:* who are you? This is your core sense of self and mission in life.
  - □ *Beliefs and values:* why am I doing this? Can be both enabling and limiting.
  - □ *Capabilities:* how do you deal with things? Skills and strategies that you use.
  - □ *Behaviour:* specific actions and reactions in your daily environment.
  - □ *Environment:* the external context in which you operate.

WHAT'S GOOD ABOUT IT
- Figure out everything you have to do: pick a time period, list all your projects, add functional things like meetings and reports and allow for interruptions.
- Work out how much time it will take to do it all.
- Write a dance card that shows what it all adds up to – you may discover that it is twice the time you actually have. Now you can do something about it.
- There are lots of ways to say no to people: question why it needs to be done, deflect some requests, delegate more, negotiate, challenge demands for your time, make people aware of the consequences.
- Deal with your guilt by stopping the sources of it and building up your resistance.
- Let stuff 'go hang'.
- When planning, say 'I'll have a look at it,' work out what you have been asked to do and the sequence for getting it

done, decide who will do what, allow for the unexpected then go back to the asker and say: 'Here's what I can do'.

WHAT YOU HAVE TO WATCH
- If you want to change your approach, you'll have to knuckle down and fill out the whole system to get a result.

How to Lead JO OWEN

WHAT THE BOOK SAYS
- This book contains all the important stuff about leading well: motivating people, building networks, selling ideas, influencing people, giving feedback, evaluating people and learning to be lucky.
- It takes you through the foundations, practice and mastering of leadership, and makes the point that leaders aren't necessarily at the top of organisations.
- The main qualities fall into focusing on people, being positive, and being professional (that means having loyalty, honesty, reliability, solutions and energy).
- Leading from the middle involves finding your way through the matrix. Those who fall by the way are: the expert (technically competent, but that's all); the cave dweller (territorial); the politician (political); the boy scout (naive); the autocrat (acts as though they already are a leader).

WHAT'S GOOD ABOUT IT
- A survey of 700 leaders reveals the qualities they look for in emerging leaders are adaptability, self-confidence, proactivity, reliability, and ambition.
- Luck is normally down to practice, persistence, and perspective.
- There are good quotes to be had here:

'Many sins are forgivable, but disloyalty is not one of them.'

'An organisation full of Ghengis Khan wannabes is unlikely to be a happy place.'

'It is possible to learn leadership. If you know how to, you are well on the way to success.'

'The successful leader will take on risk, change and ambiguity.'

- There is an interesting checklist of what people want from a good boss:
  - ☐ They show an interest in my career.
  - ☐ I trust them – they are honest with me.
  - ☐ I know where we are going and how to get there.
  - ☐ I am doing a worthwhile job.
  - ☐ I am recognised for my contribution.

WHAT YOU HAVE TO WATCH
- Not much. This is a well-organised and thoughtful book on leadership.

In Search of Excellence PETERS & WATERMAN

WHAT THE BOOK SAYS
- There are eight basic principles of how to run a successful business and stay ahead of the competition. These are:
  1. *A bias for action* – get out there and try something.
  2. *Stay close to the customer* – don't be distracted by the internal stuff.
  3. *Autonomy and entrepreneurship* – even if you're big, act small.
  4. *Productivity through people* – that's all companies are made of.

5. *Hands-on, value-driven* – top companies make meaning, not just money.
6. *Stick to the knitting* – business diversity almost never works.
7. *Simple form, lean staff* – have a simple structure and outsource a lot.
8. *Simultaneous loose-tight properties* – a combination of centralised and decentralised gives the best blend.

- Communication works best when systems are informal, intensity is extraordinary, it is given physical supports, there are forcing devices and it acts as a tight control system.

WHAT'S GOOD ABOUT IT

- There is a lot of material to work on. When they turned up the lights at Western Electric's Hawthorne plant, productivity went up. It went up again when they turned them down. In many companies management is no more than an endless stream of Hawthorne effects.
- Chronic use of the military metaphor leads people repeatedly to overlook a different kind of organisation that is more collaborative.
- The McKinsey 7S Framework shows shared values surrounded by structure, systems, style, staff, skills and strategy.
- The exclusively analytical approach run wild leads to an abstract, heartless philosophy.
- Analysing a dead fish does not tell you everything about a live fish.
- Positive reinforcement nudges good things on to the agenda rather than off it.
- Adhocracy is needed to offset bureaucracy (Alvin Toffler).
- Small groups are great chunking devices for getting things done.

- *Do it, fix it, try it* is the mantra of experimenting organisations.
- *'We don't kill ideas but we do deflect them'*.

WHAT YOU HAVE TO WATCH
- At the very least people should be aware of what the book proposes.
- The biggest criticism of it is that many of the featured companies have since disappeared. The authors' response is that they weren't writing a book called *Forever Excellent* and one can still be inspired by the good things that those companies did.
- The halo effect claims that books such as this are little more than storytelling – if it were that easy to follow eight basic principles then all companies would have done so and been a roaring success – which clearly they have not.

Leadership for Dummies LOEB & KINDEL

WHAT THE BOOK SAYS
- There is no particular philosophical stance taken – it simply guides you through all the important aspects of leadership, such as what it takes to be a leader, and how to enact it.
- You become a leader by acting like a leader.
- One of the most desirable traits of a potential leader is 'stick-to-itiveness' – patience, repetition and learning – '*Err and err and err again, but less and less and less.*' (Piet Hein)
- Imagination helps turn randomness into a vision – all leaders
need it.

- Leadership is stewardship, which means you are assuming a set of responsibilities, not getting your title carved in stone.
- The final test of a leader is that they leave behind in other people the will and conviction to carry on.

WHAT'S GOOD ABOUT IT

- There is an interesting debate around the axioms of leadership. The German word for management is *Führungskunst*, which means 'the art of leadership'. In most countries management and leadership are viewed as being different.
- 'Each one teach one' refers to the ability to spread leadership qualities around teams, although no book has ever completely resolved the issue of whether absolutely anyone can show leadership qualities or not.
- It outlines 10 qualities of a true leader: eagerness, cheerfulness, honesty, resourcefulness, persuasiveness, co-operation, altruism, courage, supportiveness, and assertiveness.
- It also outlines 10 ways to master leadership skills: preparing, volunteering, keeping an open mind, giving speeches, developing discipline, meeting deadlines, staying in touch, listening, cooperating, and doing things for others.

WHAT YOU HAVE TO WATCH

- Towards the end it veers off into a discussion about leadership in life generally. In a business context, how to lead when coaching a kids' sports team will of course be peripheral to the main point.
- It is very American in orientation, so most of the examples are US based.

Liar's Paradise GRAHAM EDMONDS

WHAT THE BOOK SAYS
- Eighty per cent of companies think that they are fraud free, but a recent survey actually revealed fraud in 45 per cent of them
- There are seven degrees of deceit:
    1. *White lie:* told to make someone feel better or to avoid embarrassment.
    2. *Fib:* relatively insignificant, such as excuses and exaggerations.
    3. *Blatant:* whoppers used when covering up mistakes or apportioning blame.
    4. *Bullshit:* a mixture of those above combined with spin and bluff to give the best impression.
    5. *Political:* similar to bullshit but with much bigger scale and profile.
    6. *Criminal:* illegal acts from fraud to murder, and their subsequent denial.
    7. *Ultimate:* so large that it must be true. As Joseph Goebbels said: '*If you tell a lie big enough and keep repeating it, people will eventually come to believe it.*'

WHAT'S GOOD ABOUT IT
- It confirms what we all suspect – that the workplace constantly bombards us with lies, fakery and spin.
- Case histories of Enron, Boo.com, the European Union and others provide proof on a grand scale.
- Deconstructions of other levels of lying help the reader to navigate their way through the day-to-day types. You can then decide how to react.
- It has tips on how to suck up to the boss, pass the buck and endure meetings.
- Everybody should read the chapter on Lies and Leadership:

'The truth is more important than the facts.' FRANK LLOYD WRIGHT

'Those that think it is permissible to tell white lies soon grow colour-blind.' AUSTIN O'MALLEY

'Honesty may be the best policy, but it's important to remember that apparently, by elimination, dishonesty is the second-best policy.' GEORGE CARLIN

WHAT YOU HAVE TO WATCH
- The book essentially condemns most corporate cultures and so needs to be viewed lightly by those who have to work in them.
- There is a moral dilemma lurking within: do you tell the truth and get trodden on, or join the liars?

Making It Happen JOHN HARVEY-JONES

WHAT THE BOOK SAYS
- Management is ultimately about people. It is an art, not a science. The artistry lies in the combination of skills, perceptions, intuitions, and combined experiences which are continually different and almost invariably unique. There are two types of manager:
  - □ The Thoughtful Manager, who is continually adding to skills and considering changes in the art form.
  - □ The Closed Mind Manager, who attempts continuously to replicate successful solutions in situations which are, almost invariably, totally different.
- There is no area of activity in the UK that does not badly need an improvement in managerial skill.
- Tasks don't get done without the commitment of those who have to execute it. Making it happen is the most

important part of any idea, and the prime management problem in any company.

WHAT'S GOOD ABOUT IT

- The author worked for ICI for 30 years, and became one of the great management gurus. The book is not a manual or a prescriptive description of the only ways in which things can be done. It is based on personal experience.
- Setting the direction is important, but how it is going to get done matters more. The people involved need to be 'switched on', and ownership of the strategic objective must be transferred to those who are to enact it – the power of good delegation. Ordering people around doesn't work well.
- Management is about change and maintaining a high rate of change. Without change nothing is possible. Whether comfortable or not, it is inevitable. The UK has a particular love of the old and a seeming contempt for the new.
- Values and beliefs in a company cannot be created out of thin air. Unless they are real, and permeate everything that is done, they will not have any effect. If they cease to be relevant they must either be abandoned or adapted to be applicable to the future.
- Harvey-Jones predicted that the future of the organisation would have to adapt to the needs of the individual, rather than the other way round. This would release energies, creativity and imagination of a different order from before. This prediction appears to be right.

WHAT YOU HAVE TO WATCH

- The book is over 20 years old and a lot has happened since. There are no sections, charts or diagrams, so it is more like reading a novel.

Nudge THALER & SUNSTEIN

WHAT THE BOOK SAYS

- The book is a discussion of how we can apply the new science of choice architecture to nudge people towards decisions that will improve their lives by making them healthier, wealthier, and freer.
- It is much loved by politicians, because it adds modernity and legitimacy to what could otherwise be criticised as blanket social engineering. The book is keen to emphasise that it is, politically, neither left nor right.
- Every day we make decisions on topics such as personal investments to schools and what our children eat. Unfortunately, we often choose poorly.
- If we take our 'humanness' as a given, we can understand how people think and design choice environments that make it easier for people to decide what is best for themselves – a nudge in the right direction without restricting freedom of choice.

WHAT'S GOOD ABOUT IT

- There are scores of examples from everyday life that make the point e.g. a director of food services in schools can increase or decrease the consumption of various foods by as much as 25 per cent simply by rearranging where they are in the cafeteria.
- Behavioural economists borrow from psychology in recognising that the mind can fool itself. In a visual context, we are quite capable of looking at two identically sized tables and being convinced that one is bigger than the other.
- The ability to be so 'smart and dumb' at the same time can be attributed to our *Automatic System* (instinct rather than actively thinking) versus our *Reflective System* (more deliberate and self-conscious).

- There is an acronym to remember the main themes:
    i**N**centives – people have to feel they are getting something for their choice.
    Understand mappings – you have to understand how they see things.
    Defaults – make sure the 'do nothing' route is one of the best.
    Give feedback – investigate the rejected options, and experiment with them.
    Expect error – humans make mistakes, so well-designed systems allow for this.
    Structure complex choices – if it's difficult, break it down into more manageable chunks.

WHAT YOU HAVE TO WATCH
- It is a 'medium' read. Some would call it heavy economic theory, others consider it to be a welcome relief from much denser academic material.

Outliers MALCOLM GLADWELL

WHAT THE BOOK SAYS
- When we try to understand success, we normally start with the wrong question. We ask *What is the person like?* when we should really ask *Where are they from?*
- The real secret of success turns out to be surprisingly simple, and it hinges on a few crucial twists in people's life stories – on the culture they grow up in and the way they spend their time.
- An outlier is a statistical observation that is markedly different in value from the others in the sample – tiny influences have made certain people 'special'.
- *Opportunity* is the first crucial element of being successful at anything. *Legacy* is the second – behaviour handed

down over many generations that dictates the way people react to circumstances.

- Countries with subservient cultures have pilots involved in more plane crashes because the co-pilots do not impose their will on their superiors – sometimes not even making emergencies evident to air traffic control.
- Easterners have a stronger work ethic and are better at maths because they are used to taking a lot of time to solve problems.

WHAT'S GOOD ABOUT IT

- Top sportsmen are born at the beginning of the year. As youngsters they start a little bigger, and are then given the best training and the most practice.
- The 10,000-hour rule shows that the best in any field have exceeded this amount of practice – those who start late at something do not usually achieve the very best.
- Studies show that social class has nothing to do with intelligence until the ability to study, revise, or practice starts to disadvantage those less privileged.
- Fans of determinism will approve of this book, since it verifies that your success is determined by where you come from and what happens on the way.

WHAT YOU HAVE TO WATCH

- This is not an academic book. It is more a series of interesting anecdotes that make a general point.
- Although it challenges you to make the most of your own potential, in reality the reader cannot change their circumstances, time of birth, where they come from, or any major factors other than pure hard work.
- The first half of the book (Opportunity) explains the origin of outliers. The second half (Legacy) seems barely related to it – it is more an explanation of cultural differences.

Purple Cow SETH GODIN

WHAT THE BOOK SAYS
- There is absolutely no point in being just like everybody else. The most successful businesses stand out because they do something different.
- A Purple Cow is remarkably different from any other product.
- The old ways of marketing are dead and being safe is now too risky.
- An *Ideavirus* is one that spreads vigorously, similar to the point made by Malcolm Gladwell in *The Tipping Point*.
- Sneezers are the spreading agents – experts who tell everyone about new products on which they are a perceived authority.
- *Otaku* is a Japanese word for something that is more than a hobby but less than an obsession. This causes people to pursue remarkable products to a level that is beyond the reason of most normal people.
- Compromise is the boring slot in any market, and all of them are filled.
- Old-fashioned, mass TV-based marketing doesn't work any more.

WHAT'S GOOD ABOUT IT
- The book is short and pithy – you can dip in easily.
- There are hundreds of examples to illustrate key points.
- It goads the reader into looking for remarkable products in their industry and beyond. These are the places where decent, original ideas will come from.

WHAT YOU HAVE TO WATCH
- Many of the things he proposes are probably easier said than done.

- All the examples are American, so have less resonance in the UK.

Screw It, Let's Do It RICHARD BRANSON

WHAT THE BOOK SAYS
- Simple truths in life, and the right attitude, can inspire and enable you to do practically anything.
- People will always try to talk you out of ideas and say, 'It can't be done' but if you have faith in yourself, it almost always can.

WHAT'S GOOD ABOUT IT
- You can read it in a couple of hours.
- The author has made plenty of mistakes and taken a lot of risks, so this is not just a 'plain sailing' manual.
- The main principles – 'have fun', 'be bold', 'challenge yourself', and 'live the moment' are solid, inspirational stuff.
- There are also much softer principles such as 'value family and friends', 'have respect for people', and 'do some good for others'.
- You can dip in anywhere and grab a motivational thought in 10 seconds.
- Choose from:
  - ☐ Believe it can be done
  - ☐ Never give up
  - ☐ Have faith in yourself
  - ☐ When it's not fun, move on
  - ☐ Have no regrets
  - ☐ Keep your word
  - ☐ Aim high
  - ☐ Try new things
  - ☐ Love life and live it to the full

- ☐ **Chase your dreams but live in the real world**
- ☐ **Face problems head on**
- ☐ **Money is for making the right things happen**
- ☐ **Make a difference and help others**

WHAT YOU HAVE TO WATCH

- The book is not particularly well-written and this is more a stream of consciousness, or a selection of sound bites.
- It always seems easier for someone who has 'done it' to reflect back on the hard times – but it is harder to apply a 'just do it' philosophy when you are actually struggling.

See Feel Think Do MILLIGAN & SMITH

WHAT THE BOOK SAYS

- Instinct is much more powerful in business than over-reliance on research or data, which can only provide you with a rear-view mirror picture.
- Focus groups and MBA models are not as good as human instinct or a passion to make a difference.
- By watching and empathising with real customers and how they act, we can evolve better ideas that solve their real needs.
- *See, Feel, Think*, Do sums up how these intuitive ideas come to fruition:
  - ☐ See: **Experience it for yourself**
  - ☐ Feel: **Empathise with your customers**
  - ☐ Think: **There is no such thing as stupid idea**
  - ☐ Do: **Make it so**
- **Why?** is a powerful question and is not asked often enough in business.

WHAT'S GOOD ABOUT IT

- This is a perfectly sound method that you can apply to any business to see what needs to be changed.
- There are scores of case histories to show how it all works (or doesn't): Carphone Warehouse, Apple iPod, Sony, Heinz, Harley Davidson, First Direct, Barclays, Geek Squad, Cathay Pacific, TNT, and more.

WHAT YOU HAVE TO WATCH

- The *Think* premise that there is no such thing as a bad idea isn't well thought out. There are clearly lots of bad ideas around.
- Whilst the process provides a framework, it isn't that remarkable. Good business people should be doing this instinctively anyway.

Six Frames EDWARD DE BONO

WHAT THE BOOK SAYS

- In a world saturated with facts and figures as never before, how do we focus our attention to make the most of information at our fingertips?
- The book suggests a 'six frames' technique to help direct our attention in a conscious manner, rather than always letting it get pulled to the unusual and irrelevant
- Just as we can decide to look north, west or even south-east, so we can set up a framework for directing our attention and interpreting information
- The six frames are:
  - □ *Purpose* – the triangle frame. To emphasise the huge importance of being clear and laying out the exact basis of your need for information.

- □ *Accuracy* – The circle frame. To direct your attention specifically to the accuracy of the information at which you are looking.
- □ *Point of View* – the square frame. To assess the information for neutrality and look at it in different ways.
- □ *Interest* – the heart frame. To direct attention to matters of interest rather than the pure need for information.
- • *Value* – the diamond frame. A summary or overview that determines the value of the information.
- • *Outcome* – the slab frame. The outcome and conclusion. Not everyone faced with the same information comes to the same conclusion.

WHAT'S GOOD ABOUT IT
- • We cannot live without information and we are surrounded by it. But it can often become overwhelming to the point where it loses its usefulness. Companies and individuals who are in this position would do well to clarify and simplify it along these lines.
- • The big enemy of good thinking is confusion, which becomes more likely the more active the mind. Clarity is good, but not at the expense of comprehensiveness. The main cause of confusion is trying to do everything at once. The system makes this an orderly process.

WHAT YOU HAVE TO WATCH
- • The book is short and simple, but it should not be applied simplistically.

Six Thinking Hats EDWARD DE BONO

WHAT THE BOOK SAYS
- In 1985, Edward de Bono introduced *Six Thinking Hats*, which has gone on to become one of the most successful approaches to business thinking in the last twenty years.
- The Six Thinking Hats are:
  - ☐ *White hat* – facts, figures, information.
  - ☐ *Red hat* – emotions, feelings, intuition, hunches.
  - ☐ *Black hat* – cautious and careful (beware overuse!).
  - ☐ *Yellow hat* – speculative positive, benefit-led, constructive.
  - ☐ *Green hat* – creative, lateral, provocative.
  - ☐ *Blue hat* – control, structure, organisation.

WHAT'S GOOD ABOUT IT
- The technique forces people to adopt different attitudes and approaches to thinking, which removes them from bias and politics.
- If followed correctly, the six hats provide an element of process to what can otherwise be a random brainstorm or ideas session.

WHAT YOU HAVE TO WATCH
- In subsequent versions of the book, de Bono noted with some dismay that the method was often used incorrectly, in that one individual often wore the same hat for the whole meeting
- Everyone should wear each hat simultaneously to make best use of everyone's intelligence and experience
- As the novelty of using the process has worn off, and business techniques have developed, the system has attracted more criticism. There may be two reasons for this:

☐ Six frames of thinking are probably too many for most people to remember accurately. (The vast majority of business people are unable to name all six hat colours, let alone their designation and function).

☐ It is hard for anyone to adopt one other mode of thinking, let alone six.

Smart Leadership YUDELOWITZ, KOCH & FIELD

WHAT THE BOOK SAYS

- The authors have three main influences; psychologists and other leadership writers, writers with unusual insights and philosophers who have pondered the human condition.
- They describe the point of leadership as being 'to initiate change and make it feel like progress'.
- Leaders need to adopt a cause but should not plan the future.
- Leadership is not always necessary – the need for it varies over time.
- Leadership is a culture, not a person.
- Managers achieve objectives – leaders work to a purpose.
- Managers defer decisions – leaders take them.
- Don't be too consensual about consensus.

WHAT'S GOOD ABOUT IT

- It is full of good advice and inspiring quotes such as:

'Leadership is a potent combination of strategy and character. But if you must be without one, be without the strategy.'

'Now that I am CEO, what am I supposed to do?'

'The only real training for leadership is leadership.'

'Leadership has a harder job than to just choose sides. It must bring sides together.'

- **The Triangle of Tensions summarises the struggle of leaders well. It includes:**
  - ☐ **The Individual Identity – who the leader really is.**
  - ☐ **The Canned Role – the formal expectations.**
  - ☐ **The Emergent Process – the messy reality.**
- **Personal mastery of this is only achieved via Learner Leadership, a never-ending circle of self-awareness, learning, judging, acting and mobilising.**

WHAT YOU HAVE TO WATCH

- **The orientation of the book leans towards money making as the desired outcome of successful leadership – this is clearly not its only value.**
- **The authors claim that it is impossible to have too much leadership in an organisation – not all would agree.**
- **There is a rather strange chapter on the value of using story-telling to encourage people to follow your chosen direction, which needs to be treated with caution.**

S.U.M.O. (Shut Up, Move On) PAUL McGEE

WHAT THE BOOK SAYS

- **Subtitled *The Straight-Talking Guide to Creating And Enjoying a Brilliant Life*.**
- **We all long for success and enjoyment but unfortunately we don't always get either of them. Have you ever thought that it might be your own attitude that is holding you back?**
- **The way you think is a major factor in determining how your life unfolds. The book shows that by taking responsibility for your life, you can fulfil your potential, seize opportunities, enjoy relationships, succeed at work and respond to adverse situations with a positive attitude.**

- You are encouraged to take an honest look at your life, remembering that it is never too late to change. We can all dump the victim t-shirt, develop 'fruitier' thinking and ditch the idea that whatever will be will be (he calls this *Ditching Doris Day*, after the song *Que Sera*).
- When you wear the victim t-shirt you become a passenger in life and allow circumstances and other people to determine your direction. Some people have become very aware of their rights, but less aware of their responsibilities.

WHAT'S GOOD ABOUT IT

- This is heavyweight life coaching with a soft centre. There are seven questions to help you S.U.M.O.:
  - ☐ *Where is this issue on a scale of one to 10?* Decide what's really important.
  - ☐ *How important will this be in six months' time?* Get things in perspective.
  - ☐ *Is my response appropriate and effective?* Choose your response.
  - ☐ *How can I influence or improve the situation?* Bring about change.
  - ☐ *What can I learn from this?* Look for learning in everything.
  - ☐ *What will I do differently next time?* Learning brings change.
  - ☐ *What can I find that's positive in this situation?* Open your mind to new possibilities.
- The way you think is influenced by your background, previous experiences, the company you keep, and the media. Faulty thinking includes being a persistent inner critic, becoming a broken record, using the martyr syndrome (when I punish me I am actually trying to punish you), and trivial pursuits (what you focus on magnifies).

- Hippo Time (having a brief wallow) is okay, so long as you snap out of it.

WHAT YOU HAVE TO WATCH
- Coaching books can sometimes be tricky. They use mnemonics to help you remember their ideas, which can come across as trite.
- The content spans personal and working life so you have to see the advice in the right context.

Sun Tzu: The Art of War for Executives DONALD KRAUSE

WHAT THE BOOK SAYS
- The ancient wisdom of this 2,500 year-old text provides invaluable commentary on such topics as leadership, strategy, organisation, competition and co-operation.
- The 10 principles for competitive success are:
  1. Learn to fight (against the competition).
  2. Show the way (leadership determines success).
  3. Do it right (all competitive advantage is based on effective execution).
  4. Know the facts (to achieve success, you must manage information).
  5. Expect the worst (do not assume the competition will not attack).
  6. Seize the day (the most important success factor is speed).
  7. Burn the bridges (position yourself where there is a danger of failing).
  8. Do it better (combine expected and unexpected tactics).
  9. Pull together (organisation, training and communication are the foundations of success).

10. Keep them guessing (the best competitive strategies have no form).

WHAT'S GOOD ABOUT IT
- It is interesting to apply the teachings of an ancient war expert to business, and in a modern context.
- The interpretations are clear and easily transferable to business matters.
- There are clear sections on planning, competitive strategy, conflict, control, positioning, flexibility and reputation.
- The overall message is: 'Do not engage the enemy unless it is absolutely necessary.' In other words, this is as much a book about the *avoidance* of war.

WHAT YOU HAVE TO WATCH
- If taken the wrong way, the whole idea of comparing war with business could lead to overly macho approaches. This is not really what the book is all about.
- There is a lot about using spies for information – this is clearly unethical.
- The book is obsessed with the competition ('the enemy'), whereas many would argue that it is more profitable to concentrate on what *you* are going to do, not what the opposition is doing.

Sway BRAFMAN & BRAFMAN

WHAT THE BOOK SAYS
- We usually think we are rational beings but the science of decision-making would suggest otherwise. Logical thought can be subverted or 'swayed' in many ways.
- Irrational behaviour can be perpetrated by the most experienced and well-trained people, including pilots and doctors.

- Common reasons are: overreacting to a potential loss, taking dangerous risks when a lot is at stake, refusing to withdraw even with a small loss, misjudging something because it is in the wrong context, and being prejudiced by prior information.
- Our brains have two particularly different parts that are constantly struggling with each other: the 'pleasure centre' wild side that gets a kick out of taking risks, shopping, winning money etc. and the 'altruism centre' that does the best for others and always seeks reasonable compromise.
- Sometimes it just doesn't seem worth the bother to dissent from the prevailing view, so many people stay quiet when the majority has got it wrong – particularly for an easier time at work.

WHAT'S GOOD ABOUT IT
- There are scores of examples from anthropology, aviation, sports and politics to illustrate the points.
- The narrative rolls along nicely – more story than textbook.
- The thesis is a useful complement to, and development of, many other social theory books of recent times: *Freakonomics*, *Nudge*, *Herd*, and *The Tipping Point*.

WHAT YOU HAVE TO WATCH
- It is this very similarity to so many other books that makes it potentially derivative. Although in theory it is original material, sometimes it feels too similar. A shorthand for separating them is:
  - □ *Freakonomics:* patterns of social behaviour can be rooted in linked causes.
  - □ *Herd:* huge numbers of people simply copy each other because they are social.

- □ *The Tipping Point:* little things can make a big difference.
- □ *Nudge:* providing different options or small incentives can change mass behaviour.
- □ *Sway:* irrational behaviour can affect even the best-trained and the most experienced people.

The Age of Unreason CHARLES HANDY

WHAT THE BOOK SAYS
- The world is changing fast, and we need to change with it. The numbers prove it, and companies and governments need to acknowledge this and think differently.
- Words are heralds of social change – by watching the way language changes, we can spot the linguistic signposts of social change.
- We work for 100,000 hours in our lives, but there are many different ways to divide this up.
- Negative capability is the ability to make mistakes and learn from them.
- Upside down thinking can make you view work as the best of the four-letter words.
- Portfolio man has five types of work:
  1. *Wage work* – money paid for time given.
  2. *Fee work* – money paid for results delivered.
  3. *Home work* – all the tasks that make a home function.
  4. *Gift work* – work done for free outside the home, such as charity work.
  5. *Study work* – training and reading.

WHAT'S GOOD ABOUT IT
- Upside down thinking forces the reader to look at things differently.

- There are many different types of intelligence, and all have value:
  - □ Analytical – the sort we measure in IQ tests.
  - □ Pattern – musicians, mathematicians and computer programmers see patterns that others do not.
  - □ Musical – those with musical skills can earn more money than conventional office skills.
  - □ Physical – e.g. sporting ability.
  - □ Practical – able to dismantle a television without naming the parts.
  - □ Intra-personal – the ability to be in tune with others' feelings.
  - □ Inter-personal – the ability to get on with others.
- The author pushes hard against 'endemic group-think', where everyone agrees with each other without thinking properly.

WHAT YOU HAVE TO WATCH
- The book is now 20 years old so certain ideas have been overtaken by events.

The Black Swan NASSIM NICHOLAS TALEB

WHAT THE BOOK SAYS
- Everything is essentially random. Black Swans (unpredictable events) disprove everything we think we know from time to time. Everyone assumed all swans were white until overseas travel revealed black ones – thousands of instances of one thing does not disprove the possibility of another. The highly expected *not happening* is also a Black Swan.
- Black Swans are near impossible to predict and yet afterwards we always try to rationalise them – an essentially pointless exercise.

- Ignore the experts, stop trying to predict everything and embrace uncertainty.
- It is easier to predict how an ice cube would melt into a puddle than guess the shape of an ice cube by looking at a puddle.

WHAT'S GOOD ABOUT IT

- It's what you haven't read, and what you do not know, that makes the difference.
- *Mediocristan* is a land where everything is averaged and so unhelpful to the point of meaninglessness. *Extremistan* is where all the learning is.
- We can learn from some important lessons:
  - □ we focus on small parts of what we know and use them to project what we don't (wrongly).
  - □ we use narrative fallacy (stories) to fool ourselves with reasons that aren't there.
  - □ we behave as if Black Swans don't exist – they clearly do.
  - □ what we see is not necessarily all there is.
  - □ variability matters: *'Don't cross a river if it is four feet deep on average'.*

WHAT YOU HAVE TO WATCH

- The book is quite long and highly technical – it is not for the faint-hearted.
- The author often veers off into anecdote.
- The author quite enjoys being obscure or obtuse.
- You cannot approach this book like a dip-in textbook.

The Halo Effect PHIL ROSENZWEIG

WHAT THE BOOK SAYS

- Much of our business thinking is shaped by delusions – errors of logic and flawed judgements that distort our understanding of the real reasons behind a company's performance.

- These delusions affect the business press and academic research, as well as many bestselling books that promise to reveal the secrets of success or the path to greatness.
- The most pervasive delusion is the Halo Effect. When a company's sales and profits are up, people often conclude that it has a brilliant strategy, a visionary leader, capable employees, and a superb corporate culture. When performance falters, they deduce the opposite but actually little may have changed.
- Other delusions are:
  - □ *Correlation and Causality* – two things may be correlated but we may not know which causes which, or whether they are linked at all.
  - □ *Single explanations* – there are usually many reasons for something, not just one.
  - □ *Connecting the winning dots* – finding similar features in successful companies doesn't help because they can't be compared accurately with unsuccessful ones.
  - □ *Rigorous research* – if the data aren't good, it doesn't matter how much analysis is done; the conclusions will still be false.
  - □ *Lasting success* – is almost impossible to achieve; almost all high-performing companies regress over time, regardless of what they do.
  - □ *Absolute performance* – performance is relative, not absolute; a company can improve and fall behind its rivals at the same time.
  - □ *Wrong end of the stick* – successful companies may have highly-focused strategies, but that doesn't mean such strategies guarantee success.
  - □ *Organisational physics* – performance doesn't obey immutable laws of nature and cannot be predicted with the accuracy of science.

WHAT'S GOOD ABOUT IT
- This is a hugely thought-provoking book that questions many pieces of received wisdom.
- The analysis of *In Search of Excellence* and *Built to Last* may force you to review your opinion of these two famous business books.

WHAT YOU HAVE TO WATCH
- Nothing. It's really worth reading.

The Logic of Life TIM HARFORD

WHAT THE BOOK SAYS
- If humans are so clever, why do they smoke and gamble, take drugs or fall in love? Is this really rational behaviour? And how come your idiot boss is so overpaid?
- In fact, the behaviour of even the unlikeliest of individuals complies with economic logic, taking into account future costs and benefits, even though they might not realise it.
- Rational choice theory affects most things, and can sit happily even with the most passionate emotions.
- Most things can be explained: overpaid (apparently useless) bosses, proximity to neighbours, racism, and divorce decisions.
- Rational people respond to incentives: when it becomes more costly to do something, they will tend to do less. In weighing up their choices, they will bear in mind the constraints on them, and their total budget. And they will consider the future consequences of present choices.

WHAT'S GOOD ABOUT IT
- The idea that everybody responds to incentives and consequences may have wider application than we think.

- Game theory (Von Neumann) uses rational decision making to analyse every decision in a way that should lead to calmer, more beneficial decisions, but it is hard for the layperson to implement. Most of us just follow the 'wisdom of crowds' principle, but don't adjust our guesses.
- Human interactions are so shot through with ambiguity that they are better viewed as focal points (Schelling): for example, everyone agrees that two people who find it difficult to meet each other in New York should meet under the clock at Grand Central Terminal at noon.
- Tournament theory means that workers sabotage one another to win the top job: the bigger the boss's pay, and the less they have to do to earn it, the bigger the motivation for everyone else to aim for it.
- 'Egonomics' is mental civil war: should I smoke or not? All humans wrestle with such conflict.
- For every year that a woman delays having her first child, her lifetime earnings rise by 10 per cent.
- The 'death of distance' doesn't make the world flatter, it makes it spikier, with evermore activity taking place in cities – centres of innovation and idea exchange.
- The rate of technological progress is proportional to the world's population – currently we should have a world-beating idea every two months (1 per billion people per year).

WHAT YOU HAVE TO WATCH
- Nothing, but don't expect any charts or easy sections.

The Seven-Day Weekend RICARDO SEMLER

WHAT THE BOOK SAYS
- The author runs a large number of companies in Brazil, and insists on working in an unconventional way.

- **The author likes to question everything:**
  - ☐ Why are we able to answer emails on Sundays, but unable to go to the movies on Monday afternoons?
  - ☐ Why do we think the opposite of work is leisure, when in fact it is idleness?
  - ☐ Why doesn't money buy success if almost everyone measures their success in cash?
  - ☐ Why does our customised and carefully crafted credo look like everyone else's?
  - ☐ Why do we think intuition is so valuable and unique – and find no place for it as an official business instrument?

WHAT'S GOOD ABOUT IT

- There are some neat little tricks that you can implement straight away, such as always asking why three times in a row.
- It provides an authoritative source on which to base radical ideas so that you can challenge staid working practices or conservative thinking.
- There are lots of ideas for maintaining staff loyalty and interest such as:
  - ☐ *Retire a little* (take Friday afternoons off and offset it against retirement age).
  - ☐ *'Up 'n down pay'* (vary hours and pay to suit circumstances).
  - ☐ *'Work 'n stop'* (take long periods off but declare an intention to return).
  - ☐ Board meetings should always have two vacancies for any members of staff that want to attend.
- One piece of reverse psychology suggests that when anything untoward happens you should do nothing on the assumption that good sense will eventually sort it out.

- There are some catchy phrases such as 'Corporate yo-yo dieting', the boom and bust cycles that companies always get themselves into.

WHAT YOU HAVE TO WATCH
- Semler has only ever run his own companies so he can only speak from comparatively limited experience.
- Semler is probably quite unconventional to work with, so not all his ideas could necessarily be implemented without causing havoc in most companies.

The Tiger That Isn't BLASTLAND & DILNOT

WHAT THE BOOK SAYS
- Seeing a pattern of stripes in the leaves, we would run from what looks like a tiger. There are illusions in numbers too, often just as intimidating. The book reveals what the numbers really show, and exposes the tiger that isn't.
- Life comes in numbers: public spending, health risks, who is rich and poor, the best and worst schools. The trick to seeing through them is to apply the lessons of your own experience, and investigate them more thoroughly.

WHAT'S GOOD ABOUT IT
- The book works through most of the manners in which numbers are presented, and shows how to make sense of them, using lots of examples from everyday news stories. Specifically relevant to business are:
  - □ *Counting* – counting things is very difficult, and the results are often wrong.
  - □ *Chance* – frequently things are truly random, but we still look for patterns.
  - □ *Up and down* – numbers go one way or the other, regardless of what you do.

- □ *Averages* – disguise huge variation and squeeze everything into a mass.
- □ *Targets* – what they do not measure is as important as what they do.
- □ *Risk* – all that matters is what it means to you.
- □ *Sampling* – if the sample is flawed, so is the conclusion.
- □ *Data* – they are often plain wrong, so be careful when drawing conclusions.
- □ *Shock figures* – are more likely to be wrong or misinterpreted.
- □ *Comparison* – mind the gap; numbers might not be comparable.
- □ *Correlation* – is not the same as causation; there may be no link.
- Everyone should read this book as a sanity check on the numbers we have thrown at us or bandy around ourselves – particularly politicians and journalists.

WHAT YOU HAVE TO WATCH
- Not much. We all have to deal with numbers, but if you don't understand them then don't misrepresent them.

The Ultimate Question FRED REICHHELD

WHAT THE BOOK SAYS
- Too many companies are addicted to bad profits. These are corporate steroids that boost short-term earnings but burn out employees and alienate customers. They undermine growth by creating legions of detractors – customers who sully the firm's reputation and switch to competitors at the earliest opportunity.
- It is possible to turn customers into promoters by asking and tracking one simple question: *Would you recommend us to a friend?* From this, a Net Promoter Score (NPS) can

be calculated. Increasing this by 12 points versus a competitor can double a company's growth rate.
- The equation is simple: P - D = NPS, where P are promoters and D are detractors. In other words, you want to have more fans than grumblers.

WHAT'S GOOD ABOUT IT
- The question is simple and based on extensive research (the author works at Bain & Co.). There is compelling evidence here that loyalty is the key to profitable growth.
- On a 10-point scale from extremely likely to not at all likely (to recommend) promoters must score nine or 10, passives must score seven to eight, and detractors must score six or below.
- Promoters are beneficial because they have a higher retention rate, margin, annual spend and cost efficiency and generate positive word of mouth.
- This system works better than standard satisfaction surveys, which fail because:
  - ☐ They ask too many questions.
  - ☐ The wrong customers respond.
  - ☐ Employees don't know how to take corrective action.
  - ☐ Too many are marketing campaigns in disguise.
  - ☐ The scores can't be linked to economics.
  - ☐ There are no generally accepted standards for them.
  - ☐ They confuse transactions with relationships.
  - ☐ Manipulation wrecks their credibility.

WHAT YOU HAVE TO WATCH
- It's a little dry, but generally very sound and worth discussing with any client who values loyalty – which should be all of them.

The World is Flat THOMAS L. FRIEDMAN

WHAT THE BOOK SAYS
- Knowledge and resources are connecting all over the world, effectively flattening it.
- These forces, which include blogging, online encyclopedias and podcasting can be a force for good – for business, the environment and people everywhere.
- There are 10 forces that flattened the world:
  1. 11th September 1989 – the day the Berlin Wall came down.
  2. 8th September 1995 – the launch of the World Wide Web.
  3. Work Flow Software – making much more stuff happen seamlessly.
  4. Uploading – everybody can contribute to online communities.
  5. Outsourcing – your company may not do much of what it sells to customers.
  6. Offshoring – many US services are provided in India.
  7. Supply-chaining – making sure everything arrives in the right place, fast.
  8. Insourcing – for example, UPS repair all of Toshiba's laptops.
  9. In-forming – Google, Yahoo! and MSN inform people at the touch of a button.
  10. The steroids – digital, mobile, personal and virtual devices all fuel the machine.
- Friedman also outlines The Triple Convergence. This is where new players, a new playing field, and new processes all come together in 'horizontal collaboration'.

WHAT'S GOOD ABOUT IT
- It is a superb synthesis of all the developments you can think of in modern communications.

- Many of the elements of globalisation are recorded in a fragmented way. Here they are all drawn together in one place.
- It is thought-provoking – so many of the developments we now take for granted happened very recently.
- There are lots of anecdotes and examples to bring the drier technological points to life.

WHAT YOU HAVE TO WATCH
- It is very long, so you need a bit of stamina to get through it.

Whatever You Think, Think the Opposite PAUL ARDEN

WHAT THE BOOK SAYS
- This quirky book explains the benefits of making bad decisions, why unreason is better than reason and how risk is the security in your life. It's about having the confidence to roll the dice.
- The problem with making sensible decisions is that so is everyone else. They are dull, predictable, and lead you nowhere. Unsafe decisions cause you to think and respond in unexpected ways.
- 'I want' is better than 'I wish'.
- It's better to regret what you have done than what you haven't.
- Too many people spend too much time trying to perfect something before they actually do it. Instead of waiting for perfection, run with what you've got, and fix it as you go.
- There is no right point of view. There are personal, conventional, large and small ones. You are always both

right and wrong. Advances in any field are built upon people with the small or personal point of view.
- What is a good idea? One that happens. One that doesn't, was not a good idea. If an idea is not taken up as a solution to a problem it has no value.
- Steal from anywhere that resonates with inspiration or fuels your imagination. Authenticity is invaluable. Originality isn't.
- *'It's not where you take things from – it's where you take them to.'* Jean-Luc Godard.

WHAT'S GOOD ABOUT IT
- The book is packed full of inspirational and contrary thoughts – just the place to start if you are bogged down or suffering from inertia.
- Until the Mexico Olympics of 1968, high jumpers faced the bar, and the record stood at 5' 8". Dick Fosbury turned his back on it and leapt 7' 4", by thinking the opposite of everyone else.
- In 1889 George Eastman invented the Kodak brand. The name means nothing but was chosen because it was short, was not open to mispronunciation, and could not be associated with anything else.
- *'The reasonable man adapts himself to the world. The unreasonable man adapts the world to himself. All progress depends on the unreasonable man.'* George Bernard Shaw
- Meetings are for those with not enough to do. They are performances, acts to convince people of their own importance.
- The world is what you think of it. So think of it differently and your life will change.

WHAT YOU HAVE TO WATCH
- Not much. This book is all about jumping-off points, so don't expect to be guided by the hand through the creative process.

Why Entrepreneurs Should Eat Bananas SIMON TUPMAN

WHAT THE BOOK SAYS
- It has 101 inspirational ideas for growing your business and yourself.
- Take positive control of your life – don't let circumstances rule you.
- The three Ps: Professional skills, Purpose, Passion. You need to be able to tick all three to claim that you are happy in life and work. If not, make changes.
- *'Nothing great was ever achieved without enthusiasm.'* Ralph Waldo Emerson.
- There are three types of people: those who make things happen, those who watch things happen, and those who wonder what happened.
- You need to see the world for what it is, examine best practice, connect with existing customers, find new ones, connect with your people if you have them and then connect with life itself.

WHAT'S GOOD ABOUT IT
- You can dip into a point anywhere. Some of the best tips are:
  - ☐ Develop a 'spoken logo' – this is your elevator pitch that goes beyond the factual and into the emotional benefit of what you do.
  - ☐ Burn your brochures – most of them serve no purpose and say the same thing.

- ☐ **Start leading or consider leaving – negative people need to move on.**
- ☐ **Ask existing customers for referrals – many people never bother.**
- ☐ **Leave the office no later than 5.30 – it's amazing what you can achieve if you do.**
- ☐ **Understand your value – too many people undervalue themselves.**
- ☐ **Keep on moving – a health point: the more you move, the healthier you are.**
- **There are lots of different forms in the appendix that you can use, such as customer surveys, self-assessments, and team performance questionnaires.**

WHAT YOU HAVE TO WATCH
- **The title is a misnomer. It is meant to catch your attention and the answer to it is simply that bananas are good for you, which is a bit of a letdown.**
- **It's not really about entrepreneurs – it is to do with anyone who works in a company.**

Why Should Anyone Be Led By You? GOFFEE & JONES

WHAT THE BOOK SAYS
- **Copying how other leaders behave will not necessarily make you a good leader.**
- **Great leaders essentially act as 'authentic chameleons', consistently displaying their true selves through different contexts that require them to play a variety of roles.**
- **Leadership is situational, non-hierarchical and relational.**
- **Leadership can come from within an organisation just as easily as from the very top.**

WHAT'S GOOD ABOUT IT

- The question in the title is the strongest point, and you should ask it of yourself if you aspire to be a leader.
- This orientation adds a dose of humility to the often macho area of leadership.
- It is easy enough to follow the steps they recommend (assuming you have the desire):
  - ☐ Be yourself – more – with skill.
  - ☐ Know and show yourself – enough.
  - ☐ Take personal risks.
  - ☐ Read – and rewrite – the context.
  - ☐ Remain authentic – but conform enough.
  - ☐ Manage social distance (tough love, and getting close but not too close).
  - ☐ Communicate with care.
- Followers are also discussed (you can't have leaders without them).
- Followers want authenticity, to feel significant, a sense of excitement and to feel part of a community.
- Leadership has a price as well as a prize – there are no easy answers, you can be easily undone, and when things go wrong it's your fault – so be careful what you pursue for the sake of it.

WHAT YOU HAVE TO WATCH

- Not much. The book is well-written and based on 25 years of research.

Wikinomics TAPSCOTT & WILLIAMS

WHAT THE BOOK SAYS

- Mass collaboration changes everything, and this is how.

- The knowledge, resources and computing power of billions of people are self-organising into a massive, new, collective force.
- Interconnected and orchestrated via blogs, wikis, chat rooms, peer-to-peer networks and personal broadcasting, the Web is being reinvented to provide the world's first global platform for collaboration.
- Peer production is what happens when masses of people and firms collaborate openly to drive innovation.
- There are many weapons of mass collaboration – free telephony, open source software, global outsourcing platforms, for example.
- Procter & Gamble now has 90,000 registered scientists who give them ideas but who are not on the payroll, courtesy of their InnoCentive marketplace.
- Companies used to be secretive. Now they can benefit from the four principles of Wikinomics which are being open, peering, sharing and acting globally.
- Wikinomics is defined as a perfect storm in which technology, demographics and global economics create an unrelenting force for innovation and change.
- The Net generation does not passively receive messages – it wants to search, scrutinise, authenticate, collaborate and organise everything. NGen norms are speed, freedom, openness, innovation, mobility and playfulness.

WHAT'S GOOD ABOUT IT

- Coase's Law from 1937 (that a firm will expand until transaction costs reach those of the open market) now needs to be viewed.
- backwards (firms should shrink until transaction costs no longer exceed the cost of doing any task externally).
- An Ideagora is a marketplace for ideas, based on the agoras that were the centre of politics and commerce in Athens.

- The benefits of peer production are harnessing external talent, keeping up with users, boosting demand for complementary offerings, reducing costs, shifting the locus of competition, taking the friction out of collaboration, and developing social capital.
- The stock of human knowledge now doubles every five years.
- Virtually all of Google's new product ideas come from the 20 per cent of time that staff are required to take off for 'goofing around'.
- Tarzan economics means that we cling on to the vine of the old before we embrace the new.

WHAT YOU HAVE TO WATCH
- It is fairly long and detailed so you have to dig hard for the nuggets.

Online resources

Fooled by Randomness, Nassim Nicholas Taleb:
www.fooledbyrandomness.com

The Black Swan, Nassim Nicholas Taleb:
www.fooledbyrandomness.com

Outliers, Malcolm Gladwell:
www.gladwell.com

Freakonomics, Levitt & Dubner:
www.freakonomicsbook.com

Nudge, Thaler & Sunstein:
www.nudges.org

Sway, Brafman & Brafman:
www.swaybook.com

The World is Flat, Thomas L. Freidman:
www.thomaslfriedman.com/bookshelf/the-world-is-flat

Wikinomics, Tapscott & Williams:
www.wikinomics.com/book/

The Ultimate Question, Fred Reichheld:
www.theultimatequestion.com

Free, Chris Anderson:
www.longtail.com

Six Thinking Hats, Edward de Bono:
www.edwarddebono.com

Six Frames, Edward de Bono:
www.edwarddebono.com

The Tiger That Isn't, Blastland & Dilnot:
www.profilebooks.com/title.php?titleissue_id = 453

The Logic of Life, Tim Harford:
www.timharford.com/logicoflife/

Why Should Anyone Be Lead By You? , Goffee & Jones:
www.whyshouldanyonebeledbyyou.com

Leadership for Dummies, Loeb & Kindel:
www.dummies.com/store/product/Leadership-For-
Dummies.productCd-0764551760.html

Screw it, Let's Do it, Richard Branson:
www.virgin.com/richard-branson/books/
screw-it-lets-do-it/

In Search of Excellence, Peters & Waterman:
www.tompeters.com

Built to Last, Collins & Porras:
www.jimcollins.com

Good to Great, Jim Collins:
www.jimcollins.com

The Halo Effect, Phil Rosenzweig:
www.the-halo-effect.com

Making it Happen, John Harvey-Jones:
www.sirjohnharveyjones.com

A *Whole New Mind*, Daniel H Pink:
www.danpink.com/whole-new-mind

See Feel Think Do, Milligan & Smith:

www.smithcoconsultancy.com/index.php/customer-experience-literature/see-feel-think-do/

Purple Cow, Seth Godin:
www.sethgodin.com/purple/

Here Comes Everybody, Clay Shirky:
www.shirky.com/herecomeseverybody/

How to be Idle, Tom Hodgkinson:
www.idler.co.uk/books/how-to-be-idle/

Execution, Bossidy & Charan:
www.ram-charan.com/execution.htm

Why Entrepreneurs Should Eat Bananas, Simon Tupman:
www.simontupman.com/author.html

Getting Things Done, David Allen:
www.davidco.com/what_is_gtd.php

S. U. M. O., Paul McGee:
www.thesumoguy.com/

BIBLIOGRAPHY

CHAPTER 1

Taleb, Nassim Nicholas. *Fooled by Randomness*. London: Penguin, 2004.

Levitt, Stephen D. and Stephen J. Dubner. *Freakonomics*. London: Penguin, 2005.

Thaler, Richard H. and Cass Sunstein. *Nudge*. London: Yale University Press, 2008.

Gladwell, Malcolm. *Outliers*. London: Little, Brown, 2008.

Brafman, Ori and Rom Brafman. *Sway*. London: Virgin, 2008.

Taleb, Nassim Nicholas. *The Black Swan*. London: Penguin, 2007.

Friedman, Thomas L. *The World is Flat*. London: Penguin, 2005.

Tapscott, Don and Anthony Williams. *Wikinomics*. London: Atlantic, 2006.

CHAPTER 2

Anderson, Chris. *Free*. London: Random House, 2009.

Edmonds, Graham. *Liar's Paradise*. London: Southbank, 2006.

De Bono, Edward. *Six Thinking Hats*. London: Penguin, 1985.

De Bono, Edward. *Six Frames*. London: Vermillion, 2008.

Krause, Donald. *Sun Tzu: The Art of War for Executives*. London: Nicholas Brealey, 1996.

Harford, Tim. *The Logic of Life*. London: Little, Brown, 2008.

Blastland, Michael and Andrew Dilnot. *The Tiger That Isn't*. London: Profile, 2007.

Reichheld, Fred. *The Ultimate Question*. Boston: Harvard Business School Press, 2006.

CHAPTER 3

Owens, Jo. *How to Lead*. London: Pearson, 2005.

Loeb, Marshall and Stephen Kindel. *Leadership for Dummies*. London: Wiley, 1999.

Branson, Richard. *Screw it, Let's Do it*. London: Virgin, 2006.

Yudelowitz, Jonathan, Richard J. Koch and Robin Field. *Smart Leadership*. London: Capstone, 2002.

Semler, Richard. *The Seven-Day Weekend*. London: Century, 2003.

Goffee, Rob and Gareth Jones. *Why Should Anyone be Led by You?* Boston: Harvard Business School Press, 2006.

CHAPTER 4

Collins, James C. and Jerry I. Porras. *Built to Last*. London: Random House, 1994.

Collins, Jim. *Good to Great*. London: Random House, 2001.

Peters, Thomas J. and Robert H. Waterman. *In Search of Excellence.* London: Profile, 1982.

Harvey-Jones, John. *Making it Happen.* London: Harper Collins, 1988.

Handy, Charles. *The Age of Unreason.* London: Arrow, 1989.

Rosenzweig, Phil. *The Halo Effect.* London: Free Press, 2007.

CHAPTER 5

Pink, Daniel H. *A Whole New Mind.* London: Cyan, 2006.

Shirky, Clay. *Here Comes Everybody.* London: Penguin, 2008.

Godin, Seth. *Purple Cow.* London: Penguin, 2003.

Milligan, Andy and Shaun Smith. *See Feel Think Do.* London: Cyan, 2006.

Arden, Paul. *Whatever You Think, Think the Opposite.* London: Penguin, 2006.

CHAPTER 6

Bossidy, Larry and Ram Charan. *Execution.* London: Crown Business, 2002.

Allen, David. *Getting Things Done.* London: Piatkus, 2001.

Maier, Corinne. *Hello Laziness.* London: Orion, 2005.

Hodgkinson, Tom. *How to Be Idle.* London: Penguin, 2004.

O'Connell, Fergus. *How to Get More Done.* London: Pearson, 2008.

McGee, Paul. *S.U.M.O.* London: Capstone, 2006.

Tupman, Simon. *Why Entrepreneurs Should Eat Bananas.* London: Cyan, 2006.

Also by the author

Marketing Greatest Hits. London: A & C Black, 2010.
Run Your Own Business. London: Hodder & Stoughton, 2010.
Small Business Survival. London: Hodder & Stoughton, 2010.
So What? London: Capstone, 2008.
Start. London: Capstone, 2008.
Tick Achieve. London: Capstone, 2008.

Index